DUMFRIES & GALLOWAY'S SMUGGLING STORY

Dumfries & Galloway's Smuggling Story

FRANCES WILKINS

WYRE FOREST PRESS

Copyright Frances Wilkins 1993

Published by Wyre Forest Press
8 Mill Close, Blakedown, Kidderminster
Worcestershire DY10 3NQ

Printed by Severnside Printers Limited
Bridge House, Upton-upon-Severn
Worcestershire WR8 0HG

ISBN 1 89775 03 5

Contents

Chapter	Page
One: Sources of Information	1
Two: History of Smuggling Dumfries and Galloway Style	11
Three: What was Smuggled?	25
Four: Where did the Goods Come From?	47
Five: The Preventives at Sea	62
Six: The Preventives on Land	77
Seven: Smugglers - The Vessels	88
Eight: Smugglers - The Men	106
Nine: Towards the Twentieth Century	122
Bibliography	

Other books by the same author, also available from Wyre Forest Press:

The Isle of Man in Smuggling History

Scottish Customs and Excise Records, with particular reference to Strathclyde

Strathclyde's Smuggling Story

Family Histories in Scottish Customs Records

Illustrations

Figure		Page
1: Dumfries & Galloway in the late Seventeenth Century	facing	1
2: Location of Dumfries & Galloway		4
3: The Stranarer area in the late Seventeenth Century		8
4: The Dumfries area in the late Seventeenth Century		16
5: Stranraer District: Residences of Early Nineteenth Century Smugglers & Their Witnesses		37
6: The East Indies in 1779		46
7: The *Flora* of Guernsey with three revenue cruisers		57
8: Creeks where Tidesmen were stationed in Dumfries		90
9: An Eighteenth Century Smuggler		103

The extracts from the Robert Morden maps are taken from the 1695 edition of Camden's Britannica

Figure 6: The East Indies in 1779 is from Vyse, Charles A New Geoghraphical Grammar

Figures 5 & 8 are from Chatterton, E Keble King's Cutters and Smugglers

The front cover is reproduced by kind permission of Imray, Laurie, Norie and Wilson Ltd and of Admiralty Charts and Hydrographic Publications

This book is dedicated to Barbara Hargreaves, whose house has been 'home' in Dumfries and Galloway for so many years.

PREFACE

In 1690 the General Convention commissioned a 'Register Containing the State and Condition of every Burgh within the Kingdom of Scotland'. The reports contained in this Register were to be obtained through a series of questions defined in the 'Instructions given by the Royal Burghs to the Visitors'. Two of these instructions were:

'6. Item in all burghs that they take exact trial into their trade, both foreign and inland, and particularly of the wines and of the vent and consumption of malt for five years backward.'

and

'7. Item that they take exact account of what ships, barks, boats and ferry boats they have belonging to them, the names of the said ships, their burden, and value of each of them, and how employed and by whom.'

The replies for Dumfries were:

'6. As to the sext article it is answered that they have had these five years bygone of foreign trade the following particulars viz one small ship from France with 18 tuns of wine and six tuns of brandy or thereby; item one other vessel from Norway with 5,000 dales [deals - timber]; item a small vessel from Stockholm loadened with iron; item one other small vessel from Bristol, of the burden 20 tons, loadened with cydar bottles, hoops and some other small goods of inconsiderable value, being four in all. And as to their inland trade they have had the particulars following viz 30 packs of linen cloth at £20 sterling the pack, in neat £1200 sterling, and other goods of that nature to the value of £480 sterling; item 5,000 sheepskins at £50 sterling the 1,000, in neat £250 sterling; item 6,000 mort lambskins, worth £17 sterling, which they sell yearly to merchants in Edinburgh and others. And that they have ten or twelve merchants shops that retails tar, lint and iron, and two shops that sells cloth and London goods; and they have some other shops of little account that sells brandy, pipes, tobacco, candle and such like wares; and three apothecaries shops. And this is all the foreign and inland trade they have to the best of their knowledge and surest information they can get. And that there is vented yearly within their burgh about three tuns of wine yearly these five years bygone, and that they cannot condescend upon what malt they consume yearly in regard their milns are rouped with the rest of their common good and that they are no further concerned than the tack duty payable to the tacksman, and that there is little malt made in the town, and that the vast part of their malt is brought from the country, and that the tacksmen of the excise are in use to set leases thereof to others so that it is not possible for the magistrates to give a true account thereof.

'7. As to the 7th article, that they have four vessels belonging to their town viz the *Adventure*, of burthen about 36 tons, the *Providence*, 20 tons, the *Concord*, 20 tons or thereby; and which three ships they value at £150 sterling, and that they have lain up these three or four years for want of trade and so are ruinous; and the *Elizabeth* of 140 tons which is lying at Kirkcudbright ruinous and disabled, so that she cannot go to sea; and that they have no other ships or boats belonging to them; and that they have a small boat about three tons, a yawl, and no ferry boat.

In comparison Stranraer had no foreign trade and their inland trade was 'most inconsiderable' and 'by retail of goods they bring to Glasgow, Ayr, Greenock and Kilmarnock from skin last they buy only knives and bonnets ...' They had no ships.

The Register was published in 1692. Within the next few years there was a dramatic expansion in trade. Almost inevitably this exposed the local dealers to the temptations of the outside world. In October 1736 the Annual Committee of the Convention of Royal Burghs sent a letter to each burgh 'representing the pernicious consequences of smuggling in its clearest light; and earnestly exhorted their countrymen to desist from so infamous a trade. Several of the burghs ... came to the strongest resolution to discourage it for the future. Viz they would not be directly or indirectly concerned in running foreign goods, or in purchasing and vending any goods knowing them to be run, but would lay themselves out to get intelligence, and assist the officers in seizing and condemning the same.'

Despite this, on 21 March 1787, the collector at Dumfries, David Staig, wrote to Mr Nish Armstrong, the head supervisor of the riding officers stationed at Newcastle, giving details of the 'pernicious practices of smuggling' in the Dumfries and Galloway area.

'I received the favour of your letter of the 9th current and shall be very happy to cooperate with you in any measure that can check or discharge the pernicious practices of smuggling. I have no doubt that these practices have been carried to considerable extent both on the coasts of Ayrshire and Galloway. Their importations are generally made in vessels of force and the cargoes deposited in places of concealment till they find suitable opportunities of removing them. Those discharged on the coast of Ayrshire are generally sent towards Edinburgh or carried across the country by Langholm towards Northumberland. The importations on the coast of Gallow, I mean such part thereof as goes towards Cumberland, is seldom carried by land, the smugglers having hiding places and associates on the borders of England, to whom they send such goods up the Firth in the night time in boats of 15 or 20 tons. And the business is begun and ended without an officer knowing of the matter till it is entirely over. I believe at Langholm there is a great deal of tobacco smuggled and manufactured under cover of one or two real certificates, taking care to have no more unmanufactured tobacco in their warehouses than corresponds with these certificates, under the protection of which they manufacture only smuggled tobacco. Last year by the order of the Board of Customs I went down with a party of twenty dragoons to Langholm and Graitney, at the first of which places I seized from one Thomas Hamilton and James Robson & Co about 7,000 pounds weight of manufactured and unmanufactured tobacco and at the latter place I seized about 3,000 pounds weight of manufactured and unmanufactured tobacco, all which has been since condemned. Langholm is about 40 miles from this place therefore I have little access to know what is transported by the carriers from that part of the country to yours. But there is an excise officer there who ought to watch over these matters. With regard to anything being transported towards England or the Borders by the carriers from this place I am persuaded you are mistaken. For I have several times had them examined and stopped when they were 10 miles advanced on the road. As I have already told you the great carriage from the coast of Galloway is by water, which is more safe and expeditious than by land.

'I understand, or at least I am informed, there is a company lately settled at Sarkfoot near Graitney, to whom the care of such goods is sent from the coast of Galloway and they transport them in their turn to the coast of Cumberland etc. But they have such hiding places underground that nothing short of a direct information can discover them. You may depend that I shall always be happy to concur with you in any measure that can discourage the practices complained of.'

This book concentrates on the development of these pernicious practices, so describing Dumfries and Galloway's smuggling story.

ACKNOWLEDGEMENTS

The author is very grateful to the Archivist, Dumfries Archive Centre, for her help, particularly with unravelling the location of 'Hopses' and to Chris Pickard, of Castletown, Isle of Man, for his introduction to the George Moore letter-books. Thanks are also due to the West Search Room, Scottish Record Office, Edinburgh; Strathclyde Regional Archives, Mitchell Library, Glasgow; The Library (Manx National Heritage), Douglas, Isle of Man and the Priaulx Library, St Peter Port, the Island Archivist and John Sarre both all in Guernsey.

INTRODUCTION

Despite the fact that possibly more has been written about smuggling in Dumfries and Galloway than any other part of Scotland, it was decided to write this book both as an essential part of the series on the Smuggling Stories of the regions intimately linked with the Isle of Man, and the subsequent series on Scottish Smuggling Stories, and as a complement to **Family Histories in Scottish Customs Records**, which is based on the Dumfries and Galloway records.

Other writers, in particular Ronald T Gibbon, Rosemary Goring and John Thomson, have looked at the Dumfries and Whitehaven custom house letter-books as a source of primary information about smuggling in the area. Before starting to write this book, it was thought that every attempt should be made to avoid any repetition of quotes taken from these letter-books. Once the work was completed, it was discovered that some repetition was unavoidable. In a few cases there is only one good example to illustrate a particular point. As a result, some re-use of what may be familiar material has been inevitable. At the same time this book also uses the letter-books from additional custom houses - Stranraer, Wigtown, Ayr, Campbeltown and Port Glasgow and Greenock - and other contemporary correspondence extracted from merchant letter-books. These sources of information are described in detail in Chapter One.

Although this is the third book using the same approach, Dumfries and Galloway stands out as a clearly defined area with a subtly different story. This is one of the main attractions of the letter-books as source material. It is possible to identify extracts from those of different areas based on the unique approach of the local collectors and comptrollers. Possibly this is inevitable as no two individuals are alike but it is almost as if the early collectors stamp the pattern on the area for the next two hundred years or more. In a study like this the individuality becomes of particular significance in the context of replies to standard circulars from the Board of Customs in Edinburgh. As a result of the details provided by generations of collectors, particularly at Dumfries, it has been possible to write the area's smuggling history through the custom house letters - Chapter Two: The History of Smuggling Dumfries and Galloway Style.

This outline history is expanded in both Chapters Three and Four, which describe some of the goods that were smuggled and where they came from, both originally and the markets or 'warehouses' established solely to supply the contraband trade. Chapter Four includes extracts from the letters of the Manx merchant, George Moore, who supplied customers in the Stranraer, Glenluce and Kirkcudbright area with tea, brandy and wine. Before concentrating on the smugglers, Chapters Five and Six describe the preventive force, who tried, at sea and on the land, to stem the flow of contraband goods. Chapters Seven and Eight look at the smugglers - a term applied both to the vessels and to those individuals who dealt in prohibited goods. Finally the story is brought into the twentieth century in Chapter Nine.

As quotes are used throughout to produce a 'They Saw It Happen' approach to the story, these have been updated in terms of both spelling and punctuation to make them more easily readable. Where words are missing, or where a brief explanation of a word or phrase is necessary, these are included in square brackets. Other brackets are in the original text. The majority of quotes come from the Dumfries letter-books so identification of these has been shortened to 'the collector' rather than 'the collector and comptroller at Dumfries'. In all other cases the collector's outport is clearly identified. In an attempt to make the story more complete and to emphasise the value of the letter-books as an information source, various themes have been maintained throughout. Examples of Robert Thomson's rum and tea smuggling produce this type of continuity.

As **The Isle of Man in Smuggling History** concentrated on what was happening on the the neighbouring coasts, there is inevitably a slight overlap in subject material between the two books. Rather than fill the text with cross-references, the reader who is sufficiently interested in smuggling should refer to the other title. Similarly **Family Histories in Scottish Customs Records** is about the people of Dumfries and Galloway and, as many of the people appearing in the custom house letter-books were involved in smuggling on one side or the other, there is also an overlap. References to this other book have been kept to a minimum for the same reasons.

Each area has a unique smuggling history, so let the people who were there at the time tell the story for Dumfries and Galloway.

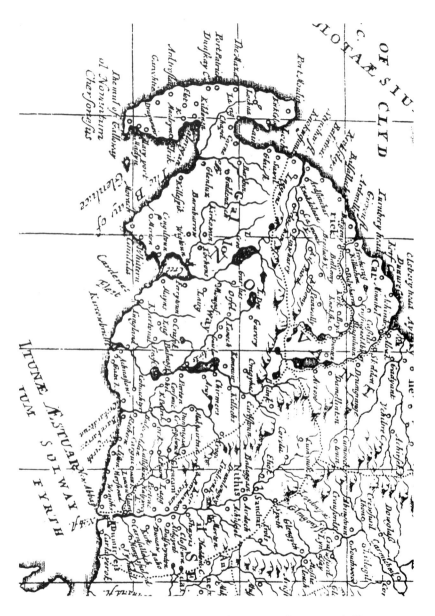

Figure 1: Dumfries and Galloway in the late Seventeenth Century

CHAPTER ONE: SOURCES OF INFORMATION

'Robert Stewart ... having discovered a small boat hovering along the coast upon the 10th (January 1711) did immediately send an express to the collector at Dumfries and also to the next officers on each hand, acquainting them of the boat and the grounds of his jealousing her for a rogue affair ... he ... did watch her all that day from eleven of the clock in the forenoon till eleven o'clock at night, still moving from place to place where he most suspected. At last the said little boat came to the very creek where he was watching, being about half a mile distant from the dwelling house of the Laird of Arbigland. He ... beholding this, lay undiscovered ... the boat ... crew, who were all strangers practiced in the running trade, set immediately to disload the boat, which so soon as ... he went to and boarded ... he seized with his [the boat's] cargo, consisting of twelve runlets [casks] containing about 10 gallons each. So soon as ... [he] had made the seizure, the boatmen all went away and left him alone in the boat. Where he stayed till about four o'clock in the morning, when the boatmen came with three horses and two servants belonging to the Laird of Arbigland. The boatmen no sooner came on board but the two of them laid violent hands on him and held ... said Robert Stewart while the other ... disloaded the cargo. Where it was carried he could not discover but does suspect that seeing Arbigland's servants and horses were present that it probably may be lodged thither or near his dwelling house.' There followed 'a diligent search ... particularly in the dwelling house of the Laird of Arbigland, where we found two ankers [casks] ... which we did seize and bring along to the custom house. We are heartily sorry that the gentlemen of the country give so much encouragement to these rogues, for if they had not their countenance, they would not dare such insults ... it's said this cargo did properly belong to them and that no merchants are concerned therein'. (Collector and comptroller at Dumfries to the Board, 11 and 14 January 1711).

This book is based on the contemporary documents which described the smuggling events from 1708 to the 1920s. The material is mainly in two forms: the official customs records for both Scotland and England and merchant correspondence, which looks at the situation from the opposite side.

Custom House Letter-books

From the viewpoint of the researcher into smuggling history the great advantage of the Union was that after 1707 the recording of customs letters became standardised not only throughout the United Kingdom but also between individual outports and the Board. The result is a series of bound books in which were transcribed the letters from the collector and comptroller at a particular outport to the Board of Customs in Edinburgh (or London) and General Orders and Specific Letters from the Board to the outports.

The early outports in the Dumfries and Galloway area, together with their Members and Creeks, are listed below.

Port	Member	Creek
Stranraer	Portpatrick	Ballantrae
		Bay of Cairn
		Scar
		Loch Float
		Drumore
		Glenluce
Wigtown	Nil	Burn of Monreith
		Isle of Whithorn
		Newton Stewart
		Creetown
		Gatehouse of Fleet
Dumfries	Kirkcudbright	Balmangan Bay
		Balcary Bay
		Entry of Ure
		Eastside
		Burbary Bay
		Carse Thorn
		Kelton
		Cummer Trees
		Annan
		Entry of Sark

The original spelling has been retained in the list, which includes some surprising places in terms of the importance of settlements along the present day coastline. Figure 1, showing the area in the late seventeenth century, and enlargements of sections of this map in Figures 3 and 4 have been included to emphasise the point.

The custom house letter-books still exist for each of the ports and are held at the West Search Room of the Scottish Record Office in Charlotte Square, Edinburgh. The Scottish Record Office have divided these letters into various different classes. Classes 1 and 2, relating to the correspondence already mentioned, are of most value. In the Dumfries and Galloway area these have survived as follows:

Dumfries (CE 51)
Class 1: Letters from the Collector: 1708 to 1883, with some letters missing during the early period. For example from 1736-1758, 1772-1778, 1792-1793 and 1798-1801.

Class 2: Letters from the Board: 1717 to 1882, again with some letters missing. For example from 1721-1724, 1749-1763 and 1789-1790.

Wigtown (CE 61)
Class 1: Letters from the Collector: 1868 to 1896 (one book only)
Class 2: Letters from the Board: 1854 to 1889 (one book only)

Stranraer (CE 77)
Class 1: Letters from the Collector: 1873 to 1896 (one book only)
Class 2: Letters from the Board: 1789 to 1909 with some letters missing, from 1792-1798.

The significance of the missing letters is that sometimes it is impossible to complete a particular story, or to compare what was happening between one area and the next. However, rather than complaining about what is missing it should be remembered that it is a miracle sufficient letter-books have survived to recreate the smuggling story of the area.

Figure 2: Location of Dumfries and Galloway

One of the earliest Dumfries letters from the collector to the Board is dated 6 December 1708. 'This is to acquaint your Honours that on Saturday last about fourteen miles from this, at a place called Carsethorn, was seized by Mr Grearson, our riding surveyor, and one of our tidewaiters a Manx boat about 10 tons burthen with three tuns of brandy and one tun of wine and some coarse Irish linen. We had information of it and that it was to be run in a creek near Abbeyholme in the precinct of Carlisle, which we informed that office of, and advised Mr Grearson to be upon his round on this coast and all our other officers to be on their guard. The bark was lying for the tide to go to that place aforementioned on Saturday last. There touched at Kirkcudbright that America merchant of Whitehaven from Virginia bound for Liverpool with tobacco ... I have given the warrant for apprehending the people that insulted the officers at Wigtown as directed ...'

Where Class 1 letters are missing, as in the case of Stranraer for the earlier period under review, it is still possible to reconstruct a situation from the Class 2 letter-books. This letter from the Board to the collector and comptroller at Stranraer is dated 28 May 1789. 'I have it in command to transmit to you for your information and government a copy of a letter from Mr Winder, one of the secretaries to the Commissioners of the Revenue in Ireland, with respect to a smuggling vessel named the *Delaware* having fired upon the *Amnesty* cutter in the service of that revenue, whereby one of the crew of the *Amnesty* had his right arm shattered very much, which has since been cut off, and received a wound in his thigh. And you and all the officers under your survey are hereby directed to use your utmost endeavours to secure the said vessel in the event of her coming within your district and in that case to detain her till further orders, giving immediate notice to the Board. And you are to communicate this information to the commanders of such of the cutters, sloops and boats in the service of the revenue of customs and excise as may arrive within your district. And in case of their falling in with the said vessel and effecting the seizure thereof, which they are to use their best endeavours to do, they are to detain her till further orders and to give immediate notice thereof to this Board.'

Because of its geographical location (Ballantrae was a creek within the port of Stranraer, although it is now included as part of the

Strathclyde region), information about the happenings in Dumfries and Galloway can also be obtained from the Ayr, Campbeltown and Port Glasgow and Greenock letter-books (held at the Strathclyde Regional Archives, Mitchell Library in Glasgow) and the Whitehaven letter-books at the Public Record Office, Kew, London. Extracts from the Liverpool books have been published by the Chetham Society of Manchester and have been used here. One letter from this source dated September 1716 refers to arms smuggling in the early eighteenth century. 'The Lord's Commissioners of His Majesty's Treasury having signified to this Board that there are at St Martin's in France a Dutch built dogger with French colours manned with Scotch, laden with salt under which are between forty and fifty chests of arms, bound for North Britain, and at Rochelle an English built vessel of about 40 tons with the figure of a woman in her head, and the like number of arms bound for the same place. You are pursuant to his Royal Highness's pleasure to seize and secure those ships if they shall arrive on your coast, giving immediate notice thereof to the Commissioners.'

Where the records for an outport no longer exist, some of the correspondence may be found elsewhere - letters from Kirkcudbright were sent to Dumfries and Liverpool and from Stranraer to Ayr and are transcribed in the relevant letter-books.

Although the Class 1 and Class 2 letters tend to dominate as source material, some information has been extracted from other classes of letter-books - Class 4 includes seizure records for Dumfries from 1867 to 1911 and Class 5 the more personal correspondence with the officers at 'Subordinate Ports and Creeks'. These creeks in Dumfries and Galloway were:

CE51 Dumfries	Annan Creek	1813-1825
	Glencaple Creek*	1825-1860
	Carsethorn Creek	1849-1855
	Kirkcudbright Creek**	1852-1884

* This includes some information about Fleet Creek
** In 1707 this was classed as a full member of Dumfries

CE61 Wigtown	Creetown Creek	1850-1888
	Garlieston Creek	1850-1888
CE77 Stranraer	Drumore Creek	1859-1889

These records have been used in considering the more modern local smuggling.

Finally there should be a comment about the Shipping Registers, which are held at Greenock Custom House. If these had existed for an earlier period (they start in 1824 for all three outports) then it would have been possible to discover the ownership of a particular smuggling vessel, for example the *Countess of Galloway*. Research continues into the shipping registers for Guernsey in an attempt to trace the ownership of the Guernsey vessels mentioned on the Dumfries and Galloway coast.

Merchant Correspondence

During the first part of the eighteenth century the Isle of Man was independent of the English crown and so able to operate under its own rules. As a result any merchant trading there was dealing in 'uncustomed or prohibited goods' legally and so was not breaking the law when selling such goods to customers in Scotland. This meant that the Isle of Man was a major warehouse for the smugglers. An accurate insight into what was happening during this period can be obtained from the letters written by George Moore, a Manx merchant, between 1750 and 1760. These are preserved in a letter-book held at the Manx National Heritage Library in Douglas. Included in this are transcripts of letters from Moore to his suppliers in Sweden, Holland, France, Spain, the West Indies and America and to his agents and customers in Scotland.

There are over thirty letters written to his contacts in Dumfries and Galloway - mainly to William Kerr in Stranraer amd John McCulloch in Kirkcudbright. The letters tend to concentrate on debts, commenting on sundry bills owing and where the money, if collected, should be transmitted. As a result they list the names of the people who owed money, so indicating those who were dealing with one merchant in the Isle of Man in the middle of the eighteenth century. These individuals are

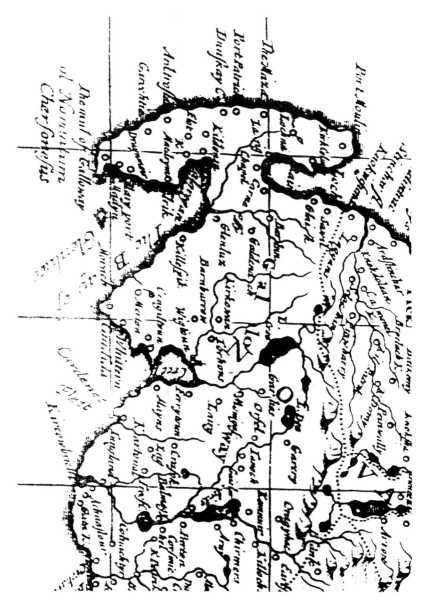

Figure 3: The Stranraer area in the late Seventeenth Century

discussed in Chapter Four. Sadly neither the Stranraer nor Kirkcudbright custom house letter-books exist for the crucial period so that other smuggling activities of George Moore's contacts cannot be traced from that source, as was possible in the Strathclyde region. But some of the surnames recurred in a list of salt smugglers in the Stranraer district in the early nineteenth century, produced for 'Family Histories in Scottish Customs Records'. Research on this topic continues.

A typical letter, dated 20 August 1755, was to Mr John McKie [writer - Moore turned to the law to recover bad debts] in Stranraer. 'You have herewith sundry bills etc as per account above which I desire you will refer to and receive the sums owing me so soon as possibly you can. I'm plagued with the old debts and am forced to give you the trouble of them. What can be done to recover any part of these pray try. When you receive value of any of said sums I desire you will let me know that I may apply the same to my occasions.'

The significance of this letter, written on 6 March 1755 to James McBride in Glenluce, is only apparent when it is remembered that the coffee was being smuggled into Galloway. 'On receipt of yours of the 30th past I caused enquiry to be made about the missing cask of coffee and find that the person it was intended by forgot taking it on board after he had lain some days windbound and was very glad to find it [the wind] was to the fore. The person from whom I had the coffee sent it down to the quay to be shipped and whether your man caused it to be put into a small cellar I have on this quay or it was put in by his order this I cannot find out, as he grudges now to receive it back. I hope you will give me directions to deliver it, which shall be done to your order. We have repeated instances of damage occasioned by the insufficiency of casks, which it is not in my power to prevent. The coopers are answerable for damages thus sustained before the boats leave the harbour but the custom has established they bear no part of the loss after the boats go out of the harbour, though but one mile, and on returning back into the harbour the damage [is] then discovered.'

Once the fiscal rights of the Isle of Man were purchased by the crown in 1765, the significance of another island warehouse came to the fore: Guernsey. Here the letter-books of the Carteret Priaulx merchant house of St Peter Port have survived and are held at the Priaulx Library on Guernsey. Similarly these include letters sent to various agents in England, Wales and Ireland, with instructions. At one stage the merchant house was considering links with southern Scotland and it is possible that at least one of the Guernsey vessels referred to in the Dumfries letters belonged to them.

These are the comments of their agent in Wales, Lawrence Banks, on the potential of the Scottish market. 'I arrived here [Anglesey] yesterday [23 April 1804] in the *Lion* after scouring the north coast [for] fourteen days. Goods was not wanted there. We parted with 300 [kegs] there on credit - drafts [promising payment] which I flatter myself are good. McDonald and Elder did not take any off us. I offered them at 3s 3d [per gallon] and they would only give 3s. The country is full of whisky or it is a good country. And in this season there is no money, no cattle selling. There will not be any goods wanted till early September and then the money will begin to circulate ...'

All this material has been collated and cross-referenced to reconstruct Dumfries and Galloway's smuggling story as vividly as possible.

CHAPTER TWO: HISTORY OF SMUGGLING DUMFRIES AND GALLOWAY STYLE

'The business of this port being chiefly to prevent running of goods from the Isle of Man, Ireland and other parts ...' (Collector at Dumfries to the Board, 24 April 1710)

The custom house letter-books discussed in the previous chapter provide sufficient information for it to be possible to trace the history of smuggling in Dumfries and Galloway from the early eighteenth century to the early twentieth century.

The relevant information is scattered throughout the correspondence in the form of responses to the Board's enquiries into the state of smuggling on the coast. In November 1785 the outports were directed to transmit 'without delay as accurate an account as you can possibly procure of the number of smuggling vessels now employed in carrying on an illicit trade in your district, stating if possible the names and size of them and the articles which they principally carry.' By the nineteenth century regular smuggling reports were submitted to the Board and the response was not always 'nil'.

The Board in Edinburgh frequently received alarming stories about the amount of smuggling carried on within the precinct of one of their outports. These stories might come either from other customs authorities or anonymous sources. In March 1783 the Board wrote 'Mr Stiles, secretary to the commissioners in London, having in his letter of the 10th inst transmitted an extract of a letter from Mr Armstrong, head supervisor of the riding officers stationed at Newcastle, stating the great increase in smuggling carrying on from the west coast of Scotland into Cumberland, Northumberland, Newcastle and the Southern Counties by an armed force ... [you are] desired to exert yourselves to the utmost of your power to put a stop to the frauds complained of.' A defensive response was inevitable.

Over thirty years later, on 4 March 1816, the Board wrote to the outports about 'the great increase in smuggling ... requiring such observations and suggestions as may occur to [them] ... for the more effectual prevention of the same within the limits of their port.'

In May 1796 the collector received an anonymous letter about the smuggling of salt at the Bardy and 'informing of a boat gone for Ireland and shortly expected to return with a cargo of salt.' He asked Captain McConnochie of the king's boat at Carsethorn to keep a strict lookout for the boat. The informer did not think that sufficient attention had been paid to their forewarning because they wrote to the Board, with more details, and this was forwarded to the collector on 26 May.

Because of the close proximity of the two coasts, Whitehaven tended to explain their problems on the uncontrolled situation just across the Border. Again the local collectors would have to justify their apparent inactivity. Finally there were the requests for more staff, or justifications to keep the 'extraordinary' [temporary] staff already in post.

The Early Days
In January 1724 the collector at Dumfries reported to the Board 'I have this day received a letter from Mr Burrow, clerk to the collector at Whitehaven, informing me that upon the 13th inst in the afternoon a small sloop came to Silloth and was there boarded by two officers who seized out of her some brandy and tobacco which was afterwards rescued from them and reshipped by a mob. And that the said sloop stood for this coast, where he suspects she may yet be skulking. Upon which I have sent in quest of the said sloop and I am resolved that if any sloop with the marks Mr Burrow gives be found in this district to stop her until I write to the collector of Whitehaven to send over the two officers that made the seizure on board the sloop at Silloth to inform me whether or not it be the same ...' There is no record of the vessel arriving on the Dumfries coast.

The Board sent the collector in June 1744 the extract of a letter which had been sent by the tobacco merchants in Glasgow direct to the commissioners of the customs at London, complaining of frauds committed at Dumfries and other places. 'Glasgow, 12 April 1744: We fair traders are much surprised at the neglect of several of the officers to let such an illicit trade be carried on by several of this kingdom and so much encouraged by those of England. We shall only mention some which to our knowledge is a very great detriment to the Government and also to us fair traders. There are three in company at Annan. The first is John Johnston, postmaster, the second is one William Hardie [and] the other is Tristram Lowther. This John Johnston is indulged by being postmaster. Hardie is brother-in-law to Mr Bryce Blair, who has a post in the government [he was collector at Dumfries], and is so much indulged by Blair that none dare meddle. Lowther is a Cumberland man and well acquainted with the officers at Carlisle. There is one John Carlyle, one of the greatest smugglers from the Isle of Man. He has a near relation, whose name is John Little. The traders in this place [Glasgow] often drink his health and tell us how kind he is to them.'

Serious attempts were being made to stop the smuggling. In 1746 the Board in London instructed the collector at Whitehaven 'to examine and report whether the sloop commanded by Captain Robinson is fit for the performance of the duty required of her, whether she can properly guard the whole of her present district in such manner as to prevent the frauds carried on by the smugglers ... or whether [if] another vessel of smaller size was provided for Captain Robinson the duty may not be duly executed and the coast properly guarded without putting the Crown to the additional expense of hiring another vessel ...'

The reply was dated 20 June 1746. 'It appears to us that the sloop now commanded by Captain Robinson is rather too large ... especially in this narrow channel up towards Silloth and Bowness, where there are many sands and banks over which the smuggling boats from the Isleman can pass at the lowest tides and the sloop only at or near the highest.

'The great running trade at present is carried on in the Borders, that is to say between Blackshaw and Redkirk on the Scotch side and Flimby and Rockcliffe on the English. And the sea here to the northward of Flimby is all the way so contracted by the land, not being above four or five leagues over, that the smugglers with their glasses can easily discover the sloop before she can make them and so steer their boats accordingly.

'That if the sloop sailed never so well and that the crew were doubled we can't believe she could properly guard the whole of her present district in such a manner as to prevent all the frauds carried on ... nor could it be done if a vessel of smaller size was provided for Captain Robinson. These coasts ... extend above one hundred and sixteen miles. And whilst he is cruising on one part frauds will be committed on another.

'The smuggling trade on this coast is altogether carried on by open boats, sharp built, very light, carries about thirty ankers brandy or rum, rows or sails well and generally five or six Manx or Scotsmen in each. On the 10th inst we see six or seven of them in a fleet ... passing this harbour, steering northward. And the riding officer at Flimby acquaints us he counted thirteen that evening together steering up for the Scotch border, <u>where they generally land without much opposition</u> and then bring the goods on horseback in a great body in the night into England, under a strong guard, well-armed, till they are passed the preventive officers on our Borders. And then they disperse all the country over, drains it of its ready money, which they carry back to Isleman and it is sent from thence to our enemies. The collector had a letter from that island of the 3rd inst that within this six weeks seven cargoes of brandy had been landed there from France and several more expected and that two cargoes of tobacco had been lately landed there but does not mention from whence ...'

On 3 September 1746 the same collector reported that he had 'information from the Isle of Man of sixteen boats being lately built or provided by the smugglers in that Island, at Ramsey, to follow the running trade on this and the Scotch border. They are each three tons, and five or six men, and are to go weekly out severally in fleets, that is two of five boats and one of six, alternately.'

It is hardly surprising that there was such a strong move by the government to curb this trade from the Isle of Man. The island's fiscal rights were purchased for £70,000 in 1765. This was believed to be a justifiable investment, considering how much the revenue from duties would increase once smuggling stopped.

Post 1765

In September 1766 the collector replied to a circular from the Board 'we beg leave to acquaint you that since the Act of Parliament for vesting the ports in the Isle of Man in His Majesty the illicit trade, which used to be carried on betwixt there and the coasts of this kingdom, is almost entirely checked and put to a stop, so far as we can learn within the precincts of this port.' In fact the smuggling from there continued, firstly ferrying the same goods brought from France and coopered off the Isle of Man and later running salt.

In the same letter the collector also replied to another circular about the Islands of Scilly, Jersey, Guernsey, Alderney and Sark 'there is no illicit trade carried on from these Islands to this port that consists with our knowledge.' The situation was to change within the next few years.

In October 1783 the collector at Whitehaven reported 'The smuggling carried on in this and the adjoining counties is generally by land and sometimes in small coasting vessels and particularly within the limits of this port from Scotland, where large armed vessels cutter-rigged, from sixteen to twenty guns are, we may justly say, constantly employed in carrying and discharging prohibited goods on that coast ...'

And on 27 December 1784 'We beg leave to observe that smuggling is not near so much practiced on this side the Solway Firth as on the opposite coast of Scotland. But we are sorry to say that of late the smuggling of geneva [gin], brandy and tobacco is carried on here to a very great height both by water in small open boats and also by land from Scotland, where we may justly say large cutters are frequently employed in bringing said commodities and landing them on that coast from foreign parts. The riding officer and waterguard within this port ... are not able to cope with the smugglers, who go in large gangs well armed ...'

In November 1785 the collector at Dumfries replied to a standard circular from the Board 'We know of no vessels in this district employed

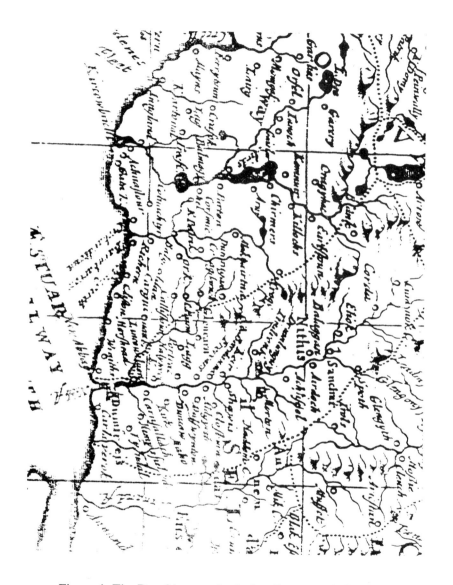

Figure 4: The Dumfries area in the late Seventeenth Century

in carrying on an illicit trade. We have no doubt a good deal of smuggling business is carried on both by land and water and principally tobacco, brandy, salt etc. But the importations we understand are generally made a good deal to the westwards of us and the quantities destined for this part of the coast, and all the way to the English Borders, are either sent up the Firth in pretty large boats or wherries or transported by horses by land. We have indeed within these few days heard of a sloop that came to the neighbourhood of the Water of Urr within these last few weeks and discharged tobacco and brandy in open day. And we wrote [to] our tidesman [Samuel Wilson] stationed in that neighbourhood if he knew or had heard anything of the matter and to give us the particulars as well as a description of the vessel and to whom the cargo belonged, if he could learn. But there being no regular post to that part of the country it may be some days before he can find an opportunity of giving us an answer. Besides the smuggling from the importations to the westward alluded to, there are also on this part of the coast frequent adventurers from the Isle of Man with boats loaded with salt and spirits. But they discharge in an hour or two and can put to sea immediately or not as they see cause.'

On 1 August 1786 the Board sent the collector a copy of an anonymous letter relating to the smuggling trade carried on in the Dumfries area. He replied 'we have reason to fear that a good deal of the information contained in the said letter is founded in fact ... The collector is going down towards the Border today and will make particular enquiry as to Mr McDowall and Company's establishment at Sarkfoot, as well as to the business in general carried on in that part of the country.'

Robert McDowall's activities at Sarkfoot are described in detail in Chapter Eight.

In October 1786 the collector reported on Thomas Geddis, tidesman, being sent to a station 'about two miles below Annan with the charge of that district to Sarkfoot, which is the extremity of this port and in which part of the coast we have no doubt a good deal of smuggling is carried on. But the whole country being in favour of the smugglers and being a lawless set of people we do not think any two or three men durst attempt to make head against them or could at least do it with any success unless there were military on the spot, always ready to support them. We do not think any of the other tidesmen could be properly spared from their present stations and therefore if your Honours judge an additional one necessary we should suppose you will appoint an extraordinary [temporary] one. But we are quite of opinion nothing can so effectually check that business as a stout boat. For if the smugglers cannot mislead an officer residing amongst them and who has no force to oppose them with effect they will certainly over awe him.

'PS Thomas Geddis has not made any report to us of any smuggling carried on under his observation since he was appointed to the station we have mentioned.'

Ten years later the collector received a copy of another anonymous letter, which he referred to the commander of the king's boat for comment. 'We have no doubt but that a contraband trade is carried on from Ireland and the Isle of Man to the quarter [Sarkfoot] pointed out and upon enquiry we understand from the Collector of Excise that the officer mentioned met with a parcel of salt, which he attempted to seize, but being in the night time and without any assistance he was beat off after being wounded in the hand. And from what information we have been able to procure, we should suppose a few boatloads may be landed there in the season. Indeed on the 11th of last month the collector had an anonymous information of a vessel being expected there with salt which was the same day [he] communicated to Mr McConnochie by express. But still we cannot think they are either in number or of the burthen stated in the anonymous information. And in support of this opinion your Honours will observe that the vessel said in the information to have lately landed a cargo of salt is stated to be of the burthen of about 30 tons but Captain McConnochie reports in his letter to have fallen in with the vessel alluded to and that by her register she was only 14 tons burthen.'

Geddis was dismissed in 1803 for having a collusive association with smugglers. When his deputation was returned to the Board in March, the collector remarked 'The station of Dornock thus become vacant ... is of considerable extent. It commences at Seafield in the neighbourhood of Annan Waterfoot and ends at Sarkfoot near Gretna, being a distance of about eight or nine miles. The services performed by this officer consisted chiefly in the loading and discharging vessels coastwise, mostly with grain and coals and occasionally a few cargoes of slate. And we have reason to believe that some smuggling has been carried on in that district in the course of the last twelve months, chiefly of salt from Ireland or the Isle of Man. And that from the extent of coast in this district it would require a steady and active young man to be an useful preventive officer ...'

The collector's comments on two other areas are of interest. In March 1787 James Hunter received a letter from the collector stating that 'Having been informed that there has been several smuggles at Southerness made by boats etc from the Isle of Man we consider it necessary for the advantage of the revenue that there should be an officer stationed there and therefore direct you to provide yourself with a house and take that station at Whitsunday first. And we strictly enjoin you to be particularly diligent and attentive to suppress that illicit trade, giving us notice from time to time of what occurs.'

When Samuel Wilson, tidesman, died in 1804, the collector wrote 'this officer was stationed in the parish of Colvend and his district extended from Southerness to Sandyhills, a distance of about six miles. And the duty performed by him during the last twelve months was in attending the loading and discharging of vessels coastwise and in doing duty as a watchman at Carsethorn on board of vessels from foreign parts. We have not heard that any smuggling has been attempted on this station since last summer, when Wilson seized a small boat that had loaded a quantity of salt from Ireland or the Isle of Man. And we are of opinion that he was of awe as a preventive officer in his district [he was eighty-seven years old when he died] and smuggling may now be attempted in this district, as the excise hulk stationed at the mouth of the Water of Urr has lately been discontinued ...'

Smuggling Methods

A letter dated 1786 from the collector summarised the smuggling methods at this period. His comment about the effect of 'taking the duty' off tea is of interest but, as has been seen already, tobacco smuggling did not actually start at this stage. 'About the time the duties were taken off the tea, the smuggling of tobacco commenced on the coast and has since continued to increase considerably, as it served as a substitute for tea to make up a cargo. For it was seldom that a cargo consisted entirely of spirits. This smuggling business is carried on chiefly betwixt Irvine and the Water of Urr ... The vessels in which these importations are made are generally freighted at Ostend or Guernsey and some small ones from Ireland and the Isle of Man. The usual freight paid on such cargoes is 20s per bale of tobacco, weighing about 120 lbs, and 10s per anker of spirits. The vessels now used in this business are in general less than they were a few years ago. And 200 bales of tobacco and 400 ankers are thought a pretty large cargo and would load of vessel ... but more cargoes are of 100 to 150 bales and of 200 to 300 ankers than above 200 bales and 400 ankers. The quantities imported within the limits mentioned has some years amounted to 4,000 bales but on an average the quantity may safely be reckoned 3,000 per annum. For there has been some cargoes consisting mostly of tobacco and it is carried for sale overland to Edinburgh, Glasgow, Paisley, Ayr etc and a good deal by water to Whitehaven and the Cumberland coast, from whence it is again carried further into the country. And a good deal that is also carried by water to Sarkfoot and that neighbourhood from whence it is conveyed to Langholm and also towards Northumberland.

'The number of sailors employed in the importing vessels are in proportion to the burthen, being from six to eighteen or twenty and their wages is 12s per week each with two guineas each per safe trip and put under no allowance as to meat or drink, having liberty to break open a cask or anker when another is done. And as a pilot is always necessary on these occasions his trouble is generally rewarded with the carriage of a certain quantity of goods freight free. Besides the smuggling from abroad a good deal of rum and tobacco is brought from Ireland. All the rum exported from Scotland to that country is returned smuggled in small quantities. And this is chiefly carried on in the neighbourhood of Kirkcudbright.

'The insurance, when any is made, on the adventures from Ostend, Guernsey etc is about 2 1/2 per cent, being for the ordinary sea risk. But it is very seldom that any insurance is made. And with regard to the time of performing one of these adventures it can generally be done in six weeks and the vessels be ready to engage in a new one.

'This is the best information we can obtain on the subject ... and it is added that the reduction of duties upon tobacco, as mentioned in the newspapers lately to be at present in agitation, would give a complete check to the smuggling of that article. And if the duties on spirits were only reduced a single year it would knock up and disperse the present band of smugglers so effectually that they would never be able to get into credit or form themselves into companies nor should it be found necessary again to raise the duties.'

The continuing reduction in duties did have an effect.

Nineteenth Century
By the nineteenth century there was a marked decrease in smuggling within the area. The responses from the collectors to standard enquiries become stereotyped.

On 26 March 1816 the collector wrote that despite the Board's fears 'after mature deliberation and advising with the inspecting coast officers, we are of opinion smuggling in this district by sea is ... very trifling, chiefly owing to there being few creeks where boats can land on account of the coast being generally flat and sandy almost the whole extent of the Dumfries-shire side of the Nith. It may, however, occur occasionally, where there is such an extent of coast to guard notwithstanding the utmost vigilance of the officers on shore of which we know no reason to doubt ...' There followed the standard request for a boat.

Three years later the collector stated 'We do not perceive or can suggest any better made than present for the suppression [of smuggling] and we do not believe any takes place in this district.'

Despite this the coast guard was established in the early 1820s and on 3 April 1822 the collector at Dumfries reported 'after communicating with Mr Lavin, inspecting commander of the district, Lieutenant Bayly, commanding coast guard at Southerness, and Mr John Dalgleish coastwaiter at Annan and Mr Johnstone landwaiter and acting tidesurveyor at Carsethorn, we are of opinion the smuggling in the limits of this port is of a very trifling nature and confined almost solely to the running of whisky (which has paid the duty) from the Scotch to the English side of the Firth, but which is now nearly put a stop to by the recent establishment of a coast guard at Bowness opposite to Annan. The officer and boatmen belonging to that station have also by constantly scouring the coast tended greatly to deter the people engaged in conveying salt illegally to the Cumberland coast, and which is made in the parish of Ruthwell, so that upon the whole we think ... that smuggling within the limits of our port is now hardly worth mentioning ...'

A year later he reported 'there has been no such thing as running of smuggled goods attempted in this district. Persons on the Border were formerly in the habit of carrying in tin cases whisky that had paid the Scotch duty across the Sark into England. But we believe this practice is greatly diminished. There is, however, a probability when the whisky upon the low duties comes into the market for consumption of it again increasing.'

Two nearly identical reports were sent to the Board in 1825 and 1826. 'We do not believe any smuggling has taken place in this district by vessels coming from foreign parts or from the Isle of Man, either before or since the coast guard was withdrawn from it, and that the illicit conveyance of whisky to the coast of Cumberland by water as well as by land has in a great measure ceased, owing to the reduction of the duty and the vigilance and activity of the officers stationed on the coast.'

In April 1828 the collector also forwarded the reports from Kirkcudbright and Wigtown. 'Though the deputy collector and comptroller of Wigtown say they have reason to believe a cutter with contraband goods was in their channel during last winter but without landing or making any attempt to land her cargo. The latter also are of opinion [with] respect to the coast guard that so large a force is unnecessary in their district, where there has been no smuggling for many years. But think differently of the revenue cruiser now stationed there, which they conceive to be very useful in checking attempts at smuggling small quantities of spirits by Manx boats in the Solway Firth and Bay of Wigtown ...'

This complacency was shaken in October 1828 but the coastwaiter at Annan believed 'no dependence can be placed on the information communicated to the Honourable Commissioners of Excise by James Bowman of Longtown relative to the landing of brandy and tobacco without payment of the duties and that the story must have originated entirely with himself without any authority for stating what he did ...' And the following day 'we have since received reports from our deputies at Kirkcudbright and Wigtown, which completely corroborate ... that from the coastwaiter at Annan viz that there has been no illegal landing of brandy or tobacco of late in the Solway Firth and that consequently the information conveyed to the Commissioners of Excise by James Bowman of Longtown is altogether unworthy of credit.'

Although smuggling continued at a low ebb, the Isle of Man was still the main supply base. Some of the regular reports are quoted below:

1830: 'For several years, with the exception of a few casks of spirits containing 50 or 60 gallons landed by an open boat from the Isle of Man, which were almost immediately seized [at Kirkcudbright] and no transactions of a similar nature has occurred since ... [at] Wigtown ... where the coast guard is still continued, there was a considerable illicit traffic carried on many years ago with Guernsey and occasionally in small boats from the Isle of Man but as it has nearly altogether ceased of late years, owing to the very general use of whisky distilled on the spot amongst the middle and lower classes and the discouragement to smuggling shown by the higher. I quite agree in opinion with Mr Simson, deputy collector, as to the inactivity of the coast guard at the Isle of Whithorn and decidedly think a small open revenue boat would afford a more efficient protection against the Manx boats, if such protection should be reported necessary hereafter.'

1831: at Kirkcudbright 'an attempt was made to land a small quantity of soap out of a vessel belonging to that port from the Isle of Man. But it was seized and condemned before the justices. And at Wigtown a farmer landing cattle also from the Isle of Man brought ashore a bottle of brandy and a bottle of gin for the purpose of dividing amongst the people who were to assist in discharging the cattle, both of which were likewise seized ...'

1834: 'the officers of the preventive boat stationed at Skinburness [England] made a seizure of about four or five gallons of Scotch whisky out of a coal sloop lying at the mouth of the river Nith in which it had been shipped clandestinely for the purpose of being illegally removed to England'.

1835: There had been no smuggling 'with the exception of three gallons of spirits mentioned in the report of Mr Innes, Principal Coast Officer at Port William ... as having been landed from a fishing boat in the Bay of Luce and brought from the Isle of Man by a person by the name of Coid, who is well known and will be strictly looked after should he attempt anything of the kind again.'

Then in November 1853 Stranraer reported 'we have reason to believe that fishermen in their boats are in the habit of having communication with vessels from foreign on their entry into the Loch whereby great facility is afforded for smuggling tobaccos and other goods in small quantities. We beg therefore to suggest that the coast guard crew at Cairn Ryan should when practicable be on board these vessels immediately on their entering the loch by which means any attempt of the kind might be prevented.'

The seizure book for Dumfries from 1867 to 1911 records only eight separate seizures. With one exception, these were of manufactured tobacco seized in small quantities, 18 lbs was the largest seizure while 1 lb was the smallest, made on ships at Barlochan, Glencaple, Kirkcudbright and Dalbeattie. One seizure of tobacco in a postal packet had to be returned because the duties had been paid.

This book tends to concentrate on smuggling in the eighteenth and nineteenth centururies, although Chapter Nine describes some later smuggling cases.

CHAPTER THREE: WHAT WAS SMUGGLED?

'Herewith please receive a certificate of the burning the following quantities of tobacco viz
4310 lbs leaf tobacco seized by William Kirkpatrick & others the 31st July & 1st August
1070 lbs leaf tobacco seized by David Staig for behoof of Robert Johnstone officer of excise the 4th December last
220 lbs roll tobacco seized by David Staig for benefit of Peter Ramsey officer of excise the 4th December last
139 lbs snuff and 201 lbs tobacco seized by John Walls the 20th December 1786
We likewise enclose the respective account of expenses thereon amounting in all to £15 12 3 ...' (Collector at Dumfries to the Board, 12 July 1787)

All the tobacco seized was burnt, following various Acts passed against that 'noxious weed', stemming from James I's great dislike of the habit of smoking and therefore of the plant itself. Other goods were 'condemned' either by the Justices of the Peace or the Exchequer in Edinburgh and sold by public roup to the highest bidder. When no bidder came forward, the goods had to be re-exposed for sale, or, when the local market was saturated, shipped to Leith where it was hoped that they would fetch a better price. This selling price was of importance as it had to cover the expenses of the seizure, appraisement to set the asking price and advertisement of the sale before the proceeds were divided between the king and the seizure maker(s).

In August 1785 12 lbs of tea, appraised at £1 10s were exposed for sale in Dumfries but 'being of a bad quality no person would give the amount so it still remains unsold.'

Each stage was carefully recorded in the letter-books. Frequently the collector merely referred to a list of seizures enclosed [and not transcribed] but where he had to seek the advice of the Board then the full details are set out from the information about an intended smuggling run onwards. Often the whole process took several years so making it difficult for a particular case to be traced through the records. The letters of George Moore, the Manx merchant, supply more intimate details of the negotiations involved in obtaining the goods and his letters are also quoted.

Although various types of goods are mentioned throughout the book, only a few have been selected for more detailed discussion here: spirits (brandy, rum and whisky), wine, tea, salt and tobacco. Several examples can be found of the smuggling of each of these commodities but only a few cases have been described in this section.

Spirits

On 28 August 1786 the collector replied to a request for details of spirits smuggling 'we have made every inquiry in our power with regard to the quantity of spirits smuggled into this district ... but the nature of the business is such and the means of procuring proper information so difficult that it is almost impossible for any person in our situation as officers, from whom every part of the business is carefully concealed, to procure an account or true state of it. We have been informed from a quarter to which we think a good deal of confidence is due that speaking in general terms the quantity consumed in this part of the country is more than three-fourths of the whole smuggled. But considerable quantities are smuggled into different parts of this district not meant for sale in it but run up the Firth towards the Borders and from there carried into the northern counties of England by land or often across the Firth to the coast of Cumberland, where there are now no boats or cruisers stationed and where we are told they meet with a ready market.

'In confirmation of this we are also informed that a vessel carried into Kirkcudbright by Captain Douglas's tender ... in April last ... had made five trips to Sarkfoot or that neighbourhood directly from a foreign part and each trip she landed 500 ankers of spirits containing about 10 gallons each. We have also been informed that a small sloop or cutter had run up to the same place very lately and had discharged 200 ankers spirits and a 100 packages of tobacco. We have been informed likewise that in the course of the summer three or four sloops or cutters, carrying about 300 ankers each, have been discharged at the Water of Urr. And all these discharges have taken place within the last six or seven months.

'We have no doubt a great deal more business has been done in the course of the last year by vessels of the same kind as well as by Manx boats smuggling in lesser quantities. But the vessels we have already enumerated are the only ones to which the information we have received applies and without some information from people having access to know these private transactions it is impossible to form any accurate conjecture of these.

'Except we have made enquiry at some of the dealers as to the price at which they can purchase smuggled spirits and find they can be bought at least a third lower than spirits of the same quality, having paid the duties. But prices vary according to circumstances. If there is a great quantity in the country they must sell low and push it out of their hiding places but if little is in the country the price is advanced in proportion.

'From the information we have been able to obtain it would seem pretty certain that upwards of 20,000 gallons of spirits have been smuggled into this district in the course of the last seven months and there seems little doubt that in the course of the year the quantity was much more considerable. But it would be perfect random work to hint at any certain extent of it. We shall be happy if this account or report is satisfactory to your Honours.'

The smuggling of brandy, rum and whisky is now discussed in turn.

Brandy
The earliest letters, dated 1708, in the Dumfries collection refer to brandy smuggling. On 12 September 1722 the collector wrote 'Upon the 10th inst we went to a place called Kirkbride about seven miles from this place in pursuance of an information of some brandy laying there and accordingly found five small casks of brandy in and about the house of one Andrew Hoatson. And after we had got it upon horse backs and brought it a small way from the house the said Hoatson raised the whole country about upon us, who came with stones clubs and firearms and

violently deforced us of the said seizure. We have inclosed a list of the persons names that deforced us with the witness names by whom we can sufficiently prove it ...'

Andrew Hoatson was involved in another brandy smuggle. On 1 October 1722 the collector reported 'the seizure of five casks of brandy by William Graham at the new house of Drumlanrig about twelve miles from this place on 26th past. It belonged to Andrew Hoatson ... for he was along with it upon the road when Mr Graham came upon with them and would certainly have again abused and deforced him had he not been so lucky as to have met that very instant with Mr Wallace of Carlisle, sheriff depute of this shire, Mr Lindsay of Mains, a gentlemen in this neighbourhood, and [the] Laird of Blackston in Renfrewshire, with his son Mr Napier, a cornet of horse, who were here seeing their friends, who all very readily gave Mr Graham their assistance. Whereupon he carried the brandy into new house of Drumlanrig, hard by the Duke of Queensberry's house, where these gentlemen stayed with him all night. Notwithstanding of all which and though Mr Graham had procured a guard of the Duke of Queensberry's tenants from Mr Daylrymple of Waterside, the Duke's factor, yet Hoatson had the impudence to attack the house in the middle of the night with about thirty fellows, armed. But they were beat off by those within and Hoatson himself was wounded in the face with a bullet. And the next morning they made a second attempt but were also disappointed. Whereupon Mr Dalrymple of Waterside and the sheriff raised as many of the country as [were necessary, who] guarded it to the warehouse here. Mr Lindsay and Mr Napier were so very kind as to come back with Mr Graham through that part of the country where he was in very [great] hazard. And the sheriff accompanied it till it was lodged in the warehouse. Your Honours plainly see by this how insolently these fellows contention the laws and that there is no doing with them but by plain force.

'I therefore humbly beg you may please to procure a party as soon as possible to this place to procure Hoatson and the rest concerned with him in the former deforcement (whose names and designations I have already sent to Mr Eyre [the Board's solicitor]) to be vigorously prosecuted. For unless they be made examples of the officers of the customs will be mobbed where ever they attempt to make seizures.

It was not until 28 October 1723 that the collector was able to reply to 'Theirs of 22nd inst with criminal letters against the persons that deforced Mr Graham and me in September 1722 and shall observe all the directions in the memorial as punctually as I can. Hoatson, the principal actor, will be ill to be found for he does not now live where he then did but is skulking through the country. However, I shall use my utmost diligence to have him personally apprehended and as soon as possible shall return all duly executed. I am confident that making these proper examples will make the officers of the customs henceforth very easy in the execution of their duty.'

By the 1750s the market was flooded with various cheap brandies. On 27 December 1750 George Moore wrote to Mr Gerard van Hoogmorf in Rochelle 'My silence proceeds from the discouragement I have in dealing in cognac brandy, the subject of our correspondence. I am nevertheless obliged to your kind advice of the currency of the market there contained in your letter ... I observe that from the poorness of your last vintage brandy at cognac is [greatly increased in price] ... and that there is no prospect of it falling this season. The price exceeds the market of this Isle, which is becoming glutted with brandy from Cette and from different parts in Spain, where the cheapness is inviting. Should any change invite me dealing at cognac I would willingly embrace under your address ...'

Rum

In November 1779 Ebenezer Hepburn, riding officer, and Andrew Newall, tidesman, stopped and seized a cart carrying 21 gallons of rum belonging to Robert Thomson 'in the middle of the day'. At first it was thought that the very openness of the transportion of the rum, together with the apparent innocence of the carter, suggested that 'no fraud had been intended'. But in December the supervisor of excise compared Robert Thomson's stock of rum with the records of his duty payments and decided that the 21 gallons must have been smuggled.

As a result the Board instructed the officers at Dumfries to have the horse, cart and rum condemned before the Justices of the Peace. The collector reported 'We had a meeting of four justices in the court house here yesterday for that purpose. But were a good deal surprised to see

Robert Thomson, the proprietor of the rum, make his appearance in the court, along with an attorney who he had employed, and claimed the rum etc. and begged to be permitted to bring a proof of its having paid all duties and that no fraud was intended, which he said he had no doubt of doing to the satisfaction of the whole court. To this the collector objected and observed to the justices that the very circumstance of its being sent without a permit was a sufficient cause for its being condemned as the Law was very clear on that point. And that he did not think that the justices had the power of dispensing with the laws ... However, they differed from him and said that where circumstance appeared favourable for the accused party they had a power of mitigating or even dispensing with the laws. After hearing both parties, the justices adjourned to Thursday the 7th of January next, when they allowed all parties to summon witnesses and bring proof of the several things alleged. In this case we beg leave to request that your Honours will give us your directions how to conduct ourselves and whether or not we should employ an attorney for behoof of His Majesty or whether you would choose to have the information withdrawn from before the justices and have the cause tried before the court of Exchequer, if this can now be done, which we are not masters enough of the law to judge of. But whatever you direct we shall to the best of our abilities execute and we beg you will give us directions in this affair as soon as you conveniently can.'

When no reply was received the collector wrote on 31 December. 'As we will not have an opportunity of writing to you again after this day's post so as we can receive an answer before the trial comes on we give you this trouble, begging you will consider our former letter on this subject and give us such directions there anent as you shall think proper. We have likeways been thinking it might be of use to have the oath of the carter sent out here to produce in court and if you are of the same opinion you will please transmit it. We likeways beg to know if the justices determine in favour of Robert Thomson if it is your pleasure that the goods be immediately delivered up to him or if any appeal can be made to the court of Exchequer or other superior court and if such appeal can be made whether or not you will choose us to make it, all which particulars we beg your Honours answer to ...' The rum was delivered to Thomson.

Whisky

In contrast to the brandy and rum, the whisky which was smuggled into England was always home-produced.

On 5 January 1820 John Dalgleish reported from Glencaple to the collector at Dumfries 'for the information of the Honourable Board that George Brown and William Elliott, tidesmen, inform me that a number of persons both of the Scotch and English side of the water are in the habit of carrying whisky in tin cases from this neighbourhood into Cumberland. That they collect in great numbers with arms and threaten death to any officers who might attempt to stop them and seize the spirits. From the inimical disposition of the people in general to assist the officers and the total inability of two or three officers to make seizures under such circumstances, I am afraid [there is] nothing effectual to stop the progress of the practice of these smugglers without military aid, as it is always under cloud of night and particularly in dark moons when they follow these illegal practices. And I may mention that Mr Lang, the excise officer here, concurs with me in this opinion.' There is more about the smuggling of whisky in Chapter Eight.

Wine

Wine was being smuggled from France, Spain and Portugal from the early eighteenth century. In March 1724 the collector reported 'In our search after ... goods upon the 24th we found at Battlehill, a place close upon the shore within a mile of Annan, 21 hogsheads of red decayed wine, which we judged to be the product of France, hid in a barn to which we were refused access until we threatened to break open the door. We seized the same and carried it to Annan and have lodged it there in a vault under the tollbooth, which we have rented from the magistrates, for we could not get carts to bring it to Dumfries. Neither did we think it safe to bring it so far over the country. The wine is very indifferent and we are at a loss to find out the merchant's design in running so much bad wine into the country. But if they have had any indirect views in laying it in our way we shall take all imaginable care to disappoint them. We will send your Honours samples of every hogshead with the first carriers that you may be judges of the quality and give the necessary orders for the appraisement thereof ...'

In May 1724 there were two further seizures of wine including three hogsheads of white and one of red at Graitney and 17 hogsheads 'all very good' at Kirkbean.

An anonymous letter dated 27 July 1785 informed the Board of four hogsheads of wine sent from Ayrshire to Mr Schaw [also spelt Shaw] in Thornhill. 'And we direct you to send an intelligent officer to examine the cellar therein mentioned (taking care to proceed according to law) and upon finding any wine for which it shall not appear that there is legal credit to secure the same for our directions.'

'Upon their arrival there they were refused access to Mr Shaw's cellars. This obliged them to break open the doors and [they] found four hogsheads and one pipe of red port wine ... Mr Shaw delivered into the custom house in March 1784 a certificate for two pipes of condemned red port wine from Ayr but no mark was upon said certificate whereas the pipe brought here is marked upon the bung BB and is much larger, which gave them every reason to believe that it was not the identical wine. Therefore they likeways secured it and one hogshead of Lisbon ...' Thomas Twaddel, landwaiter, and Baldwin Martin, tidesman, were offered a bribe by Shaw and were obstructed by the postmaster and others in making the seizure 'which they at last effected by the assistance of Mr Leonard Smith, officer of excise, and a party of military.'

The Board commented 'We highly commend Mr Twaddel and Baldwin Martin for their judicious and resolute conduct upon occasion and as Mr Smith, excise officer's, assistance was given at so critical a time we think him in justice entitled to an equal share with the seizure makers and likeways the military to the same allowance, as if they had been present at making the seizure, and have allotted to the informer a third of the officers' share ... and we have also directed the solicitor to commence prosecution against Mr Shaw for the treble value of the wine seized for receiving and harbouring the same and also to prosecute him ... for £500 for attempting to bribe the officers. The conduct of the postmaster is under consideration.'

In December 1785 Hugh McCornock junior, comptroller's clerk, served a subpoena upon Shaw. His expenses were one guinea. The trial was set for June 1786 but at the last minute Shaw agreed to pay a fine and so the witnesses had to be recalled. The collector reported 'it was too late to send an express after Mr Twaddel, he being upwards of four hours gone. We however immediately dispatched Hugh McCornock junior ... to Thornhill and through the country to stop the different witnesses and he is now returned, having countermanded all them in that country as well as them in Dumfries and demanded their tickets from them, except Robert Kirkpatrick, postmaster in Thornhill, who had transmitted his to Edinburgh along with a certificate which was thought proper to take from him. Mr McKennel merchant here being gone from home his ticket could not be got but so soon as he comes home he shall be acquainted that his attendance is not necessary and his ticket shall be taken up ...'

Tea

The other beverages considered can all be looked upon as luxuries but even tea, which is now taken for granted, was smuggled because of the high prices and duties payable on this commodity.

On 23 September 1753 George Moore sent a letter to Messrs Bagge Wilson & Hall in Gothenburg 'I wrote to you the 5th instant for three chests of bohea, three chests of singlo, one tub of hyson tea, six quarts and six china pint mugs to be forwarded by the first opportunity for this Isle, the value to be drawn for on Mr Abraham James Hillhouse, merchant in London, and desiring you would write him for causing insurance be made on the value until safe landing here. To this I refer you. I'm now to own receipt of your letter of the 22 July, which has been mislaid and therefore till now unanswered. I observe you expect the prices of tea will be low this seaon, which may be of benefit to me in said small commission I have addressed you. I desire you will also purchase and send me by the vessel with the said tea about £20 worth of china cups and saucers of different sorts, the lowest price, value whereof let be added to the tea invoice, the value to be drawn for and insured in the same manner as the tea ...'

This letter was to be forwarded to Gothenburg by Mr James Crosbie, merchant in Liverpool, who was to debit the postage to Moore's account. It is possible that this tea shipment is referred to in a letter discussed in the next chapter.

Robert Thomson appears again. In 1777 John Graham, tidesman, seized a parcel of tea which was subsequently claimed by Thomson. The Board's solicitor was suspicious because there was no evidence that Thomson owned the tea at the time of seizure 'but had become claimant to avoid giving testimony in the cause ... the said Robert Thomson having thereupon sworn that the property belonged to him at the time of seizure he cannot be required to give evidence. And that as the matter at present stands there is no other witness of the facts proposed to be proved by the defendant but the carrier. And it appearing to us improper to bring the seizure to trial on the single testimony of the carrier, we therefore in order that the said John Graham may appear as an evidence have directed the solicitor to enter a nole prosequi to the information of seizure exhibited in his name and to acquaint you when he has so done, whereupon the tea in question is to be reseized and returned by either of you [the collector or comproller] provided you are not the persons to prove the time at which the permit for the tea in question was first produced at the custom house by one Mr Anderson. And in that case any other officer in your option may reseize the goods, care being taken specially to mention in the return that the officers' share in case of condemnation is to be applied to the incidental superannuation fund, except such part as may be adjudged reasonable to be allowed to the person who shall reseize the tea for his trouble.'

The tea was reseized by the collector, condemned the following February and sold in March 1778 for £17 15s.

Salt
This is another basic commodity which was smuggled to avoid duties. There were two different methods. Either the salt was brought in directly from Ireland or the Isle of Man or it was relanded after being cleared, and bonds given, for the herring fishery. On 18 January 1777 the collector was informed 'Application having been made to the Board by the proprietors of the salt works on the east and west coasts of Scotland representing that most of the families on the coast from Greenock to Stranraer are supplied with Irish made salt to the great prejudice of the revenue and the said proprietors ...'

In November 1793 an anonymous information about salt smuggling at Annan was sent to the Board. 'It may be proper to mention to your Honours that it is matter of general surprise that in this quarter of the country no attention is paid to a material branch of the revenue, the salt duty. I think it may be asserted with certainty that from Dornock Burnfoot about two miles below this burgh to Sarkfoot, about six miles further down the Solway Firth, the Government loses in duty upon salt upwards of £3,000 per annum.

'In open boats of six or seven tons salt is constantly landed ... chiefly from the Isle of Man. And so open is that trade become of late that it is exposed to sale so publicly in different places along that coast, as in other parts by the fair trader, and no notice being taken of it. Most all the two parts in the Border are supplied with it as also a considerable quantity carried over to the English side adjacent, where your Honours know the duty is considerably higher than the Scotch.

'I am told the officers of the revenue do not chose to interfere in this matter as making seizure of it occasions much trouble and little or no profit, sometimes loss. Surely it is of consequence to look into this matter, which the writer asserts to be truth and cannot be denied. But the way to put a stop to it he shall not presume to dictate but in the meantime as a company of Fencibles are now in this quarter thereby a spirited officer might do a good deal to put a stop to it. And if the salt seized was allowed to be sold by auction at or near the place where seized it perhaps might be sufficient inducement to the active ...'

In March 1794 John Martin junior, fish curer at Dumfries, cleared out 244 bushels English duty free salt in the *Nith*, John Ewart master, for the British white herring fishery. 'But he gave Ewart instructions to reland the salt and to proceed to Ireland and there take in an equal quantity to be used on such fish as he might get or bring back, in the event of getting fish. And that the said salt was relanded accordingly about Dalbeattie or the Water of Urr ... and there sold in a clandestine manner. But Ewart was not able to fulfill the latter part of his instructions by bringing an equal quantity from Ireland ...'

The story is continued in a letter from the collector at Ayr dated 8 December 1794. The *Nith* had been seized there and he had to explain the delay in taking her dimensions. 'These ... could not be taken sooner as the vessel has until the 5th inst been mostly under water, occasioned by the great floods. And in answer to that part of your Honours said order requiring to know if proof can be had of the importing of the salt in this vessel from Ireland and her being commanded during the voyage by John Ewart, the master, and to ascertain the quantity of salt so imported and the value thereof, we humbly acquaint your Honours that ... [all this and] that the quantity so imported was nine tons can be proven by Donald Murchy and Donald Shaw, residenters at Kildonan in Arran, and David Bodden and William Bodden, residenters at Turnberry. And that the usual value of salt when landed here is about £6 per ton, being £54 the nine tons.'

The following March the collector at Dumfries went down to Glencaple and examined John Ewart, now late master of the *Nith*. He believed that Nathaniel Sloan, mentioned in Ewart's oath, and some others in his neighbourhood might be able to provide further proof of what had happened but as 'they live at some distance from this and in a different county the examining of them will be attended with some expense ...'

The case ran into difficulty because the Board wanted the bond entered into by Martin to certify what he was going to do with the salt and the customs blue book, which would record the shipping of the salt for the fishing but could not be found. The landwaiter, Mr Waddell, was now dead and a diligent search was to be made for the book, for which the surveyor was held responsible. However, sufficient evidence was produced because in August 1795 a writ was directed to the sheriff of the county of Dumfries, returnable the 24th November, against John Martin junior in Preston, Stewartry of Kirkcudbright.

On 24 December 1813 Sir John Reid, commander of the *Prince of Wales* cutter wrote to the Board about the suppression of salt smuggling from Ireland to Kirkmaiden, following an information sent to them from Stranraer. He went to Drummore, where he found two of the three boats mentioned had returned, presumably loaded with salt. One was laid up

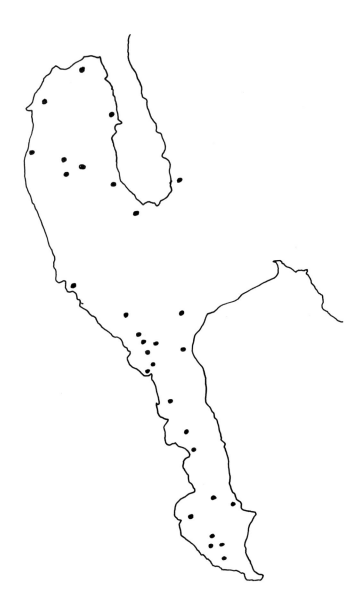

Figure 5: Stranraer District: Residences of Early Nineteenth Century Salt Smugglers and Their Witnesses

and detained by Mr Kerr, the local tidesman, one had gone back to Ireland, where it was sold, and the third had been sold in Ireland 'and therefrom did not return.'

'From everything I could learn of smuggling in that district of salt I found it was very little of late and what was smuggled was always in small boats, whose cargoes never exceeded forty bags or two tons, which boats there is hardly a possibility of getting hold of at sea as they are so small and their passage made always at night. That they never can be discovered from any vessel and the instant they see a vessel, of which they can do before they can be seen, they take down their sail till she passes to prevent such discovery. I am fully convinced that without the aid of the excise on shore the salt smuggling in the district of Kirkmaiden will never be got completely under. The population of that district is by no means great and the salt smuggled into it now only for their own consume, which might certainly be stopped if the excise officers were to visit and inspect the stocks of salt in each farmers's possession. And whatever quantity of Irish salt found to be seized and the possessors prosecuted before the justices for the whole of the penalties. And the difference between Scotch made salt and Irish is so very well known that there could be no difficulty in such determination. That very few examples would have the effect wished for and without something of this kind it follows the smuggling of salt from Ireland to that part of the coast will not be put a final stop to.'

A chapter in 'Family Histories in Scottish Customs Records' is dedicated to the salt smugglers of the Stranraer district in the early nineteenth century. It is unnecessary to repeat the list of those involved here. Figure 5 indicates the residences of these individuals.

Tobacco

The smuggling of tobacco into the west coast of Scotland was a major occupation, which involved at least as many people as the salt. But the smuggling was at a different level. Whereas the salt tended to invlove the end user, and being a bulky/perishing product it was not then smuggled inland or across the Border in large quantities, the tobacco smuggling involved merchants who had a built-in organisation to dispose of it. A brief note of explanation is necessary. The tobacco was often imported legally and certificates of duty having been paid obtained by these merchants. They then received a drawback or debenture for all the tobacco, manufactured or unmanufactured, which they subsequently re-exported. It is at this stage that most of the smuggling took place.

In March 1724 the collector wrote 'I think it my duty to lay before the Honourable Board anything that comes to my knowledge that may contribute to the discovery of frauds in the revenue, though it should not amount to a legal prosecution against the persons concerned in these frauds. Wherefore I have sent you inclosed an account (which I have obtained) of all tobacco imported into the Isle of Man from 24 June 1723 to the 25 December following with an account subjoined of all tobacco entered outwards for that Island for said term from this port [Dumfries] and member of Kirkcudbright not contained in the said account of importation, by which you will plainly see that there are 127 hogsheads which have been entered outwards from this port ... to that Island and for which the merchants have received debenture (besides the 45 hogsheads that Mr Lutwidge entered outwards in the *Larchmere,* that have not been carried thither but without all manner of doubt have been relanded somewhere in Britain) and I make no doubt but it will be found the same way at other ports upon comparing the entries outwards with this account of importation to the Island.

'Your Honours will observe by the inclosed account that Mr Lutwidge hath got an entry for 50 hogsheads in the *Larchmere* shuffled into the collector's books of that Island. But I must observe he hath concerted this affair wrong for that ship took only on board that voyage nine hogsheads and one barrel of tobacco at Whitehaven and 45 hogsheads at this port, which in all makes 54 hogsheads and one barrel. But by this account there have been landed out of her 50 hogsheads in the Isle of Man and there were on board when she stranded nine hogsheads and one barrel, which make 59 hogsheads and one barrel so that there have been four hogsheads on board more than were entered outwards either at Whitehaven or this port. I heartily wish that all the measures he takes to conceal the fraud committed by him about these 45 hogsheads may be as ill concerted.

'I have an account from that Island that about the latter end of December last there came a small bark into Ramsey Burn from Kirkcudbright with about 22 hogsheads of tobacco on board and that she stayed there till the 14 February last, when she took on board a boatload of brandy, which was sailed from Douglas to her and then sailed for some place on this coast, without putting one hogshead of her tobacco on shore in that Island.

'I have acquainted the officers of Kirkcudbright with this account and have made what search I possibly could for her in this district but can get no account of her. I am persuaded it is the *George of Parkgate*, Samuel Gray master, for she carried out 21 hogsheads of tobacco from Kirkcudbright about the latter end of December last. It was part of the *Queen Ann*'s cargo belonging to Mr Lutwidge for which he hath received payment of the debenture. And I do truly think that now to prevent that inconveniency of stopping their debentures the merchants are falling upon this method of letting their ships lie in the Isle of Man till the thirty days expire after sailing from their port here that they may get payment of their debenture and then run it back in the same bottom to some place of Britain by which practice they likewise save the duty payable in that Island.'

The rest of this section deals with one smuggling case. It started in March 1786 with a letter from the Board in London to Edinburgh inclosing 'a copy of a paper of information of illicit practices carried on upon the Borders of Scotland by several persons manufacturers etc of tobacco'. The Board directed 'the collector, Mr Douglas, surveyor general, with the assistance of such officers as they can best trust ... to proceed forthwith to the places mentioned and examine the possessions of James Robson, Thomas Hamilton and - Ferguson ...'

The collector's report dated 14 April gives a summary of what happened. 'The collector, Mr Douglas ... and Mr Twaddel, landwaiter, proceeded towards Graitney, taking with them a party of a sergeant and twelve dragoons from Annan. And having arrived at Ferguson's house they immediately set about examining his stock. But having reason to suspect from several circumstances that notice was sending to different parts of the country they judged proper to leave Mr H McCornock junior, the comptroller's clerk, who accompanied them, with George Halliday, tidesman, and two dragoons to take an account of Ferguson's stock and to guard it till the return of the party from Langholm to which place they set off immediately.

'Having got to Langholm the party ... divided and entered the houses of James Robson and Thomas Hamilton. In Robson's house were found 1018 lbs leaf, 2514 lbs stalks, 92 rolls containing 545 lbs and 134 lbs snuff making in all 4211 lbs and in comparing that quantity with his certificates ... there apprehend an excess of 1250 lbs and his whole stock was consequently seized.

'Here it may be proper to take notice of the very extraordinary quantity of stems. By the two certificates for unmanufactured tobacco which he produced the whole number of pounds including both leaf and stem were only 2035. Now as we are informed the ordinary proportion of stems in a hundredweight of unmanufactured tobacco is only about 20 lbs. It follows therefore of course that as the half of his 2035 lbs leaf tobacco was only manufactured there could be no more than 181 lbs stalks in that quantity in the proportion we have mentioned and it follows also that having 2514 lbs stalks he must have manufactured a very large quantity of tobacco for which no certificates can be produced.

'In Hamilton's house was found 891 lbs leaf, 633 lbs stems, 504 lbs shag and 483 lbs roll tobacco, making together 2511 lbs, which was considerably under the quantity contained in a certificate which he produced. But said certificate having little appearance of authenticity his stock was seized under the idea that it [the certificate] was false and fabricated. On examining it, which your Honours will be pleased to do, you will observe the figure '4 hogsheads' has evidently been altered and the whole written part of it seems to have been executed with the same hand.

'The term 1/5 days given to carry the tobacco from Leeds to Langholm is much too short, the distance being one hundred and fifty miles. And it is not common to express the same any other way than in writing. Indeed in the way 1/- stands in Hamilton's pretended certificate it might be made 15, 25 or 50 days, as he found it convenient. When examined as to J Lee, the pretended officer, he said he understood him to be an excise officer at Leeds. But in short from every circumstance the certificate was considered fictitious and from a full persuasion of that being the case the tobacco was seized.

'While this business was carrying on both Hamilton and Robson and the populace (who were very numerous) behaved decently and offered no insult to the officers or party but threats and insinuations. Having been heard to drop from some worthless fellows it was thought advisable before the tobacco was attempted to be removed to send privately for another party of six dragoons, who were stationed at Ecclefechan about 45 miles from Langholm, and everything was then conducted without disturbance. But without the military we are pretty certain very little or none of the tobacco would have left Langholm, as the officers would not have got any person to give them assistance. Nor would carts have been procured. Indeed foreseeing the difficulty after the seizure was made and secured by the military it was found proper that one of the officers should go to Longtown (about 12 miles from Langholm) and engage a wagon.

'On the party's returning again to Graitney and examining Ferguson's stock it appeared he had on hand 2135 lbs leaf, 657 lbs stalks, 251 lbs roll and 8 lbs shag, making in all 3051 lbs. It appeared also from the four certificates that he had purchased and brought from Glasgow since the 9th of April 1785 of manufactured tobacco 3138 lbs. So the stock appeared rather short of the credit. But then it was discovered that 26 rolls weighing about 150 lbs had been abstracted during the time [we] had been at Langholm, which would have made up an excess. Besides Ferguson must have been in the practice of making some sales during the year of manufactured tobacco. But his quantity of stalks convict him. For it would appear from his having on hand 2135 lbs in part of 3138 lbs leaf, which he had brought with certificate from Glasgow, that he had only manufactured the difference, being about 1000 lbs. And taking the stalks ... as the aforementioned proportion of 20 lbs in the hundredweight he should only have had about 180 lbs in place of 657 lbs, the quantity found in his custody. It is evident therefore that he must have manufactured and have had much more tobacco through his hands than certificates can be produced for. Under all these circumstances it was judged proper to make the seizure and we hope the whole procedure will have your Honours approbation. Since the tobacco was lodged in the custom house it has been carefully weighed and your Honours will receive an account thereof enclosed, by which you will see the whole quantity seized is 9773 lbs neat and each person's property is kept perfectly distinct and separate.

'The distance of Langholm from this place being upwards of forty miles and the party being considerable, together with the nature of the service, rendered the expenses very heavy and an account of which will be furnished by the collector so soon as your Honours may have had the matter under consideration ...'

The Board instructed the collector to check out Hamilton's certificate and there followed a long correspondence with John Sturgess, the collector of excise at Leeds. 'A few weeks ago some of the officers of the revenue made a seizure of a considerable quantity of tobacco at a place called Langholm in the Borders of Scotland. And when on that service a certificate was presented by one Mr Thomas Hamilton of that place for four hogsheads unmanufactured tobacco, weighing 4236 lbs, which it appeared by said certificate had been sent from Leeds to Langholm on the 20th December last and was said to be a part of the stock of Mr J Berwick.

'Several suspicious circumstances appearing on the face of the certificate, the tobacco under his protection was detained till its authenticity could be established. By Mr Hamilton saying he believed the person who signs the certificate as an officer of the revenue and whose name is J Lee to be an excise officer I give you the trouble of this to enquire whether there is any such officer and whether he granted the certificate in question. This with any other information you can give me on the subject will much oblige.'

In May the collector reported that he had received a reply from Leeds 'having no doubt it will satisfy you that said certificate is perfectly false and fictitious.' The Board was not entirely satisfied because he then wrote 'they desire me to write you again requesting information whether at the 20 December last there was any officer of excise or customs by the name of J Lee doing duty at Leeds. The certificate in question is evidently fabricated but the commissioners wish to have every satisfaction in their power. And therefore as you said in your last that no certificate was granted for the removal of tobacco by any officer of excise on the 20 December last they desire further to know whether you derived your information as to that particular from the books of office or from what other source. I beg your answer in course ...'

On 19 July 1786 the Board wrote that 'upon considering the sundry papers on this subject we direct that the tobacco be returned for condemnation making a separate return for each dealer's parcel without loss of time so as the seizures may be brought in this term in the court.'

The report of the tobacco being burnt is dated 18 April 1787. '5669 lbs tobacco, 134 lbs snuff and 3743 lbs of tobacco stalks seized by Mr David Staig [collector], David Douglas surveyor general, Thomas Twaddel landwaiter and George Halliday found at Langholm, Longtown etc £88 2s 8d ...

'Disallowed £31 18s 1d for personal and military expenses, as not being charges of seizure.

'Allowed to pay:

- to two constables at Langholm for assistance	14s
- for bags to carry rappee etc	14s
- to George Johnstone for weighing the tobacco	12s
- to John Wright for the carriage of the tobacco from Langholm etc	£8 13s 0d
- to Harkness for carriage of tobacco from Graitney	£2 0s 10d
- to Hugh McCornock for sundry horse hire bills etc	£2 12s 11d
- to George Johnstone his account for weighing	£2 13s 0d
- to apprizing	£2 2s 0d
- to warehouse rent	£2 2s 0d
Total allowance made on seizures at Langholm etc	£22 3s 9d.

'The amount of the articles disallowed for the support of the military in making the seizure at Langholm, Longtown etc being £31 18s 1d, as mentioned in the foregoing part of this letter, you are to deduct from the seizure makers allowance of £88 2s 8d and to divide the remainder, being £56 4s 7d among the officers mentioned in the return of seizure ...

'The military charges exceed the eighth of the officers' allowance, which they would have been entitled to if they had paid their own expenses, but as they did not and that the said expenses are deducted out of the officers' reward there is nothing due to the military.'

The next chapter considers the supply bases for these smuggled goods.

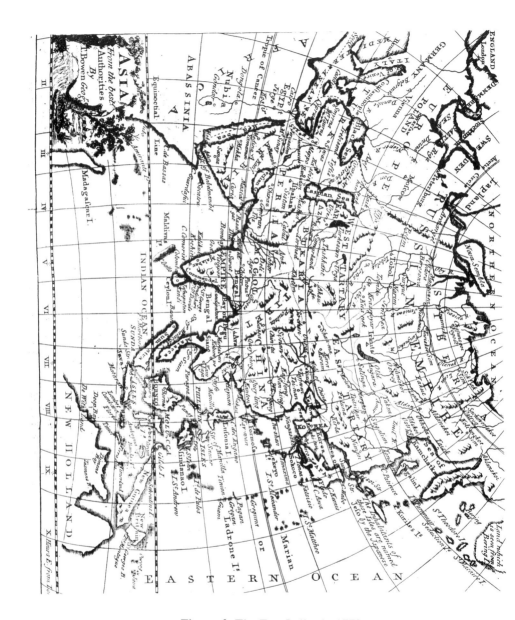

Figure 6: The East Indies in 1779

CHAPTER FOUR: WHERE DID THE GOODS COME FROM?

'We understand, however, from authority which we think can be relied upon that in the course of last year computing from 5th July 1790 five cargoes were imported as under:

1st a sloop from Guernsey, name the *John and Mary*, carrying about 350 packages of tobacco and spirits the different quantities of each not known but may be valued at £1200 or £1300

2nd the same sloop another trip, taken by Captain Cook off Annan, loaded with 1071 gallons brandy, 177 gallons rum, 549 gallons geneva, 8837 lbs tobacco and 679 lbs tea appraised at Kirkcudbright at £1310 12s 9d

3 a brig from Guernsey supposed to carry 700 or 800 packages but the different species not known but believed to consist of a sorted cargo of tobacco, rum, brandy and geneva [gin] and may be valued at £1900 or £2000

4 a sloop from Ostend, name unknown, carrying 350 or 400 packages of a sorted cargo the contents unknown but valued at £1200 or £1300

5 a cutter from Ostend, name the *John and Jenny*, carrying also a cargo of tobacco and spirits the different species unknown valued at £1300

Total £7210 12s 9d.' (Collector at Dumfries to the Board 16 August 1791)

    The collectors received constant informations about contraband goods headed in their direction from areas as close as the Isle of Man, Sanda and Rathlin, virtually within sight, and from further afield. Some of these goods did not originate in Europe but came from the East Indies (see Figure 6). The English East India Company held a monopoly on goods imported from that area - tea, spices and materials. This meant that they could control the prices, keeping these high even before the duties were applied. Several East India companies were set up in Europe, some specifically to supply the Britsih smugglers. Others were more than willing to pass on their tea imports, as this beverage was not popular on the continent. This explains why goods were smuggled from Gothenburg and Ostend.

The local islands - the Isle of Man, Sanda and Rathlin, acted as entrepots where goods could be held until the conditions - weather, dark nights and position of revenue cruisers - were perfect for a run to the mainland.

The Isle of Man
Chapter Two has explained the role of the Isle of Man so this section concentrates on the George Moore correspondence. He wrote over thirty letters to his contacts in the Stranraer-Glenluce-Kirkcudbright area. The names included in these letters are listed below:

John Agnew,	McCree, Glenluce
Robert Agnew	Hugh McCulchin
David Alexander	John **McDowall**, High Port Nessock
John Blair, Gagbory	Thomas **McDowall**, Port Nessock
Cairgawne	James McFearran, Kirkmaiden
Gal Cochrane	**McGaa**
John Cochrane	McKiand
Donaldson	Ms McKie
John Donnan	John McKie, Stranraer
Mrs Ferguson	Alexander **McMaster**
James Forans	Andrew **McMaster**, Sandmiln
Andrew Hannah	John **McMaster**
James Hannah	John McNellie
John Jameson	Jenny **McTalderagh** [McTalderoch]
Andrew Kerr, Wigtown	Pat **McTalderagh** [McTalderoch]
William Kerr, Stranraer	Jane McTar
Kilpatrick	Samuel McTier & Co
David **Leggatt**, Glenluce	Pat Nibloe
John Mair	Mary Port
James McBride, Glenluce	Laird of Shenan
McBrigart	Charles Well
John McClure	

Where known, the residences have been included on the list. The surnames highlighted in bold appear on the list of salt smugglers and their witnesses in 'Family Histories in Scottish Customs Records'.

Moore tended to use John McCulloch in Kirkcudbright as postman, enclosing letters for Edinburgh and London. Often these were not the only copy. On 6 November 1750 he wrote to John Snell in London 'Above is copy of my letter to you of the 30th ult by way of Kirkcudbright'.

William Kerr played a more significant role and was frequently required to collect outstanding bills and 'if you can raise a sum' to transmit it to either William Snell, Abraham James Hillhouse or Richard Oswald, all merchants in London or Messrs Peter and John Murdoch, merchants in Glasgow.

The actual sums of money owed by individuals were impressive. John Jameson £37 5s 3d and a second bill of £51 11s 6d; James McBride £19 13s 3 1/2d; Samuel McTiar and Co bills of £30 2s 5d and £23 6s 9 1/2d and John McMaster £59 6s 9 1/2d. Some of these bills were of long standing - John McNellie had a bill for £14 6s 8d from May 1744, one of the earliest dates associated with Moore's smuggling trading activities.

Even the Laird of Shenan was overdue in his payment. As Moore explained to John McKie, his writer [lawyer] in Stranraer on 7 July 1752 'you will therein find a missive whereon I delivered some goods to the order of the Laird of Shenan. A balance hereon is still owing me and it grudges me in looking over my books to see that it remains unpaid. It is a long time since but I hope it is not yet out of his remembrance nor do I think he will rest the delay of payment arising from an accident, whatever that did happen to the wine, as he is well acquainted that my demand for the payment is founded on the delivery of the goods here at the then selling price with me. On finding this missive pray in my name ask the payment of the balance thereon due me. If payment is refused I hope he will not take it amiss that I direct you [to] use the legal diligence for recovery thereof, which I desire you will accordingly use or cause to be done for me.' As Moore undertook a legal trade, he resorted to the law to reclaim his outstanding debts.

On 20 November 1752 Moore tried to placate William Kerr, who was concerned about debts owing both to McKie and to himself for services rendered. 'I observe what you mention about Mr McKie's services to me and yours this last summer. I received from him £2 1s in part of Pat Nibloe's debt owing me. Nibloe still owes me £4 0s 8d. I think this was the only article that Mr McKie had account with me for in the last year and as Nibloe's debt still partly lay over I did not advert to making any mention about satisfying Mr McKie, intending this to rest until Nibloe had fully discharged his debt. Before the last year I remember Mr McKie recovered some debts for me. The sum was small. I desired him to let me know what I was to pay him for his trouble and I think he made a note thereof, which I paid him. I must own to you that I would be well content to make satisfaction to any of my friends who are so kind as to transact my manner of business for me and if in any instance I have omitted this with respect to Mr McKie it would give me pleasure if he let me know of it. For on every occasion I shall cheerfully satisfy any trouble I give him.

'As to making you any allowance, your remark is very just, which has been owing to an accident you did not attend to ... However to make amends in this instance I have sent you with the bearer, Robert Agnew, a bag containing two dozen of white port and a bag containing two dozen of red port. Please accordingly accept. For the future I think our accounts should be mutually to our satisfaction so it would be best that the premium for your trouble be fixed. Whatever charges you lay out in receiving money for me, namely postages or expresses, let this be charged to my account and I'm further willing to allow you one pound for each hundred pound you receive and remit. If herewith you be satisfied please let me know.

'And as to Mr McKie who continues disposed to oblige me in this way let me with freedom direct the diligence to recover any debt owing me and let a charge be made in his bill or note of charges to satisfy himself for his trouble, which I refer to him and desire he may make as occasion from time to time may require.

'If herewith you and Mr McKie be satisfied, our correspondence this way may increase rather than diminish.'

Extracts from some of the other letters are quoted below:

19 February 1754 to William Kerr, Stranraer: 'I received the favour of your letter dated the 5 December whereby I find my debtors are quite neglectful and decline paying the sums they owe me. I am still of the mind that ultimate diligence is necessary for by this means only can I expect to have satisfaction. Since I received your letter I have been waiting an opportunity to send you the tea you write for but no Kirkmaiden boat has yet been here.'

4 December 1754 to John McKie, Stranraer: 'The backward payments I now meet with from my customers about Stranraer give me the highest reason to be displeased with my dealing with them so that as they deserve no favour let me beg that for recovery of one and all my debts you will use or cause to be used ultimate diligence. I desire you will remit what money you can get for me to Messrs Richard Oswald and Co merchants in London.'

6 March 1755 to John McKie, Stranraer: 'With respect to what is owing me in sundry old and new accounts pray do for me as you would for yourself. John Donnan has not paid me a farthing. He was tother day in this town but slept out of it without giving me an opportunity of seeing him and I missed him before he left this Island. I would not send you any tea by Mr Cormick for there is none in town anything like as good as what you had last from me. Robert Agnew and Cochrane I'm afraid I shall lose by. The rest I hope will in time. I'm surprised John Mair has not paid his bill yet. He laid out my money in the building of a boat. Surely he should be compelled to make me satisfaction.'

3 January 1756 to John McKie, Stranraer: 'I've received your letter of the 3rd last Nov and agreeable therewith I have delivered to the bearer, John McDowall, four bags wine for which as above your account is debited £5 6s 8d. I hope the quality will meet your approbation. I'm sorry to see you have had no success in getting the value of any of the bills due me. I have accidentally met with John McDowall in this Isle and held him to secure the value of what he owes but he respectively says that he has paid you. If so it must have been following the date of your letter or if he has not paid you I expect he soon will.'

It is still unclear exactly how Moore set up his smuggling contacts on the Scottish mainland but he maintained them through regular visits. For example in July 1752 he refers to catching the wherry at Port Nessock. 'Until I was leaving Port Nessock I had some hopes of seeing John Jameson but he did not return ...'

Finally there is a brief insight into George Moore the farmer. To 'assist his stock' he had decided 'that Scots milk cows will best answer me ...' In March 1751 he wrote to Andrew McMaster in Sandmiln 'I have therefore to desire you'll look out and buy for me six cows and a young bull. The cows I would have one for the rumar milk so that the first of them to calve ...'

Sanda and Rathlin
Other islands were subsequently used as depots for smuggled goods both by the Irish and French smugglers. The following extracts come from the Campbeltown letter-books.

On 9 March 1789 the collector wrote to the Board 'The accounts we daily receive from several channels of information, on some of whom we can safely rely, of the alarming height to which smuggling is carried on to and from the Island of Sanda within twelve miles of this harbour towards the Mull of Kintyre, we think it our duty to lay before your Honours. The Breakenridges of Redbay in Ireland have, we are assured, taken this Island as a central situation for the conveyance of their smuggled goods from Ireland to the coast of Ayr ...'

In December 1791 the collector, surveyor and boatmen set sail with the custom house boat by eleven o'clock at night of the 20th current in the prosecution of it [an information] ... relative to Rathlin ... at about twelve o'clock when they perceived a cutter which they took to be one of the revenue cruisers but on approaching her, she then lying at anchor to the north-west at Ushent Bay at the island of Rathlin, found her to be a large smuggler piercing nine guns of a side, appearing to be at least long six pounders. Having hailed her no answer was received than her hailing us also and piping all hands on deck. [They] declared if we did not bring to and come to an anchor along side of her they would sink us. About half past two o'clock of that day they ordered us to make sail and keep by them.' This undignified voyage continued until four o'clock that afternoon 'when ... they again hailed us and ordered us to loose up to the wind, which we did, and shortly thereafter directed us to keep to leeward of them. And then desired we might make the best of our way to Campbeltown. They then hauled their wind about four leagues to the west-south-west of Sanda and ... so long as we could perceive her she continued ... steering for the Galloway coast. About five pm lost sight of her and got to an anchor at Sanda. The night dark and the gale increasing we continued there till next morning in anxious expectation of getting to Loch Ryan to give intelligence of this cutter being on the coast. But a very severe gale caused us to run for this port and we now write to the Collector and comptroller of Stranraer giving them information and describing the vessel as follows:

'An English built cutter by appearance of about the length [of] Captain Crawford or Captain Hamilton's cutter and equal in beam. With a topmast on end struck down but the rigging ... the copper for the gaff at the upper part of the mast appeared nearly to surround it and another copper a considerable distance below the same did not surround the mast near so much as the other. She had three blocks at the mast for the peak part, which makes three bolts through the mast head, with the standing part of the halyards made fast to the gaff. Her bowsprit runs through the bow of the larboard side of the stern and her tiller cut hauler serves for a bobstay and ... same side through a hole close by the hawser hole with an knick each side if the stern head below the black stroke to secure the stem ...' After all, they had had plenty of time to observe her.

Guernsey

With the purchase of the Isle of Man, Guernsey took over much of the former Manx trade. Again the collectors would receive information - in April 1789 via London of several smuggling vessels now loading at Guernsey with tea and tobacco which are intended to be run on the coast of Scotland or Ireland.

Then in December 1789 'Good information has been communicated to this Board that on the 12th November last there were lying loaded at Guernsey ready to sail for Scotland and Ireland with the first fair wind no less than fourteen sail of smuggling vessels:

Donner Willie for the Cloan
a large lugger for the Cloan, no guns on board
Taylor and Neil for Red Bay and Rathlin in Ireland and the Isle of Sanda in Scotland
Alexander of Ballycastle for the Rathlin in Ireland
Craig for Ladyburn or Ballantrae
a large cutter of 20 guns for Rush and the mountain part in Ireland
Port Lee for the Cloan
and six wherries for Rush and the Skerries in Ireland

'It appears that Taylor's vessel is arrived and has been seized since smuggling her cargo but it is thought none of the other vessels have yet landed.'

It is unclear in this context whether or not 'the Cloan' refers to the Clone company at the head of Luce Bay.

One of the problems over trying to trace the Guernsey vessels is that ships calling at Guernsey are referred to as 'from' there whilst they may in fact have been owned and mastered by non-Guernsey crews. Despite this there follows a list of some of the more frequently mentioned 'Guernsey' masters and vessels which appeared in the Dumfries and Galloway area.

Masters
It is interesting to note that all the examples quoted below come from the Stranraer letter-books as Galloway, from its very location, tended to be more exposed to the Guernsey smugglers.

Captain Doyt: On 8 November 1803 the Board commented on a letter from the collector at Stranraer that 'information was received about a smuggling lugger, commanded by Captain Doyt, from Guernsey, which had made her appearance on the evening of the 3rd current off Clanyard Bay and you having stated in the postscript to your said letter that you would have informed the revenue cruisers but they being under admiralty orders you thought it would be of no service.'

Thomas Goulder: On 16 July 1789 the Board wrote to the collector at Stranraer 'Having under consideration your letter of the 14th inst stating proceedings had by you and the other officers with regard to a smuggling lugger commanded by one Thomas Goulder, which vessel discharged her cargo consisting of tobacco, tea and spirits at the bay of Auchinmalg in your district on the night of the 10th and morning of the 14th inst, we acquaint you that a proper watch should have been set so that a constant lookout might have been kept both night and day, Auchinmalg being the known seat of smuggling and where it was to be supposed she would return, as she did. And we direct that you do make particular enquiry and report whether it was owing to fatigue that both Mr Williamson and the tidesman went to bed, as stated in your letter ... for if one of them had continued on the lookout it might have answered the purpose of apprizing you of the return of the smuggler so as to have prevented the completing of the smuggling.'

In December 1790 the Board reported 'You have positive intelligence that the *Queen* smuggling cutter, [Thomas] Goulder commander, is now on her way from Gothenburg with a cargo of teas to be run on your coast. And that the lugger mentioned in the Board's order of 24th of October last is now loaded at Guernsey and intends also to smuggle her cargoes on your coast, which intelligence you state has been communicated to the commanders of the *Royal George* and *Prince William Henry* cutters, both then lying at Loch Ryan and waiting for a favourable wind to carry them round to the Bay of Luce. I have it in command to direct you to give notice of this matter also to any ships of war or admiralty cutters that may be in your district and also to the commanders of any excise cutters that may be there. And you are to make it your business to know how the commanders of the *Royal George* and *Prince William Henry* cutters conduct themselves upon this occasion.

The following December the Board referred to a seizure of tobacco and spirits by the comptroller and other officers 'landed in your coast out of the *Queen* cutter, Goulder commander, from Guernsey.'

Kennedy Scott cannot be traced in the Guernsey records and has been described as 'an outlaw' so that it is unlikely that he was a Guernseyman. On 9 October 1790 the Board warned the officers at Stranraer that the principal offiecrs at Looe had received an information that a lugger called the *Ceres* of Guernsey mounting sixteen carriage guns, Kennedy Scott master, was to sail that day from Guernsey for some port in Scotland laden with 1200 ankers of spirits and a large quantity of tobacco.

Jack Yawkins and his exploits are described in Chapter Seven.

Vessels

The following vessels are all named in the records as being clearly connected with Guernsey. Often nothing came of a forewarning from the Board but where the vessels were subsequently chased and/or seized this is discussed in greater detail in Chapter Seven: Smugglers - The Vessels.

Betsey

The *Betsey* was a brigantine registered in Guernsey in July 1790. The following year she was seized and sold at Dumfries, where she was registered de novo in early 1792. Her story is told in detail in Chapter Seven.

Charlotte & Ann

Although there appears to be no clear evidence that this vessel was a smuggler, when she reported at Kirkcudbright from Guernsey with thirty-one pieces of Portugal wine to discharge at Balcary in June 1785 the surveyor general, David Douglas, was instructed to get there as soon as possible to supervise her discharge.

Flora

This Guernsey vessel is pictured in Figure 7. Her story is told in Chapter Seven.

Hawk

On 4 April 1789 Mr Carmichael, commander of the king's boat at Carsethorn, was informed that by information 'received by this day's [post] it appears that the *Hawk* lugger was lately loading in Guernsey a cargo of contraband goods. Also an American brig called the *Washington* and a small black cutter, name unknown. The cutter is loading a cargo of best teas and bound either for Ireland or Scotland ...' The *Hawk* was frequently used by the merchant house of Carteret Priaulx but there are

Figure 7: The *Flora* of Guernsey with three Revenue Cutters

no appropriate letters for this period. Jack Yawkins's vessel was also called the *Hawke*.

Lyon
On 7 September 1802 the collector and comptroller at Wigtown 'acquainted the Board that the *Lyon* smuggling cutter has been at anchor upon 6th inst about 11 o'clock in the morning in the Bay of Float on the west side of the Bay of Luce, supposed to be from Guernsey, with smuggled goods on board, and that she is described as having a gaff topsail and painted yellow sides and that they communicated the above intelligence to you; I have it in command to direct you to report what you have done in consequence thereof.' As this letter was sent to Stranraer there is no record of their response.

In late September 1802 the Carteret Priaulx *Lion* was making a delivery of goods to customers in Cornwall but no record has been found of what she was doing earlier in the month.

Mayflower
In July 1791 the collector received a letter via London from principal officers at Guernsey 'stating that the ship *Mayflower* of Fowey is now fitting up for a lugger at a small harbour about three miles distant from the town. That she will be ready for sea in a month and will sail for the north-west coast of Scotland with tobacco and tea and also that the lugger was lengthened 15 feet and is expected to carry some arms.' The *Mayflower* discussed in Chapter seven came from Larne.

Queen
This was Thomas Goulder's vessel and is mentioned in the previous section.

Stag
In December 1791 the Board in London forewarned of 'intelligence received [that] a cutter called the *Stag*, supposed to be licenced with fourteen four-pounders and twenty men, will sail in a few days from Guernsey to the west coast of Scotland with a cargo consisting chiefly of tobacco'. This information was passed on to Stranraer.

Research into the ownership of these vessels continues.

Ireland

Although Ireland cannot be considered as an off-shore island in the same context as those discussed above, she did play a very similar role in acting as a temporary warehouse.

In October 1796 the Board received information that 'a lugger called the *Shuffleboard*, commanded by Doyle a Rushman, pierced for sixteen guns but carries only a few swivels and navigable with eighteen men, intends landing a cargo of spirits and tobacco on the coast of Scotland or Ireland.'

The collector and comptroller of Douglas in the Isle of Man wrote to the Board in March 1794 with infomration that 'the ship *Levant* of Liverpool, bound with a cargo of staved salt from thence to New York, on her passage outwards stuck a rock on the coast of Ireland and was brought into that port on the 13th February much damaged. That what remains of the salt (they suppose about 10,000 bushels) is now landing and selling by public sale, which not being fit for fishery they have reason to believe will be bought with a view to smuggle it on the coast of Scotland.'

Ireland was also a major supplier of salt in its own right. The problems of deputations will be discussed in the next chapter. These arose because of the geographical location of Dumfries and Galloway. In October 1796 Hugh McConnochie, commander of the king's boat at Carsethorn, seized at the Border 'the smack *Nancy & Jean* of Larne with 14 tons of salt, which he has given in charge to the collector and comptroller at Carlisle. And I have it in command to acquaint you that the vessel and salt will fall to prosecution in England or Scotland according as the offence of importation of the salt was committed in one or the other, which does not clearly appear ...'

In October 1803 the collector received a letter from the Board 'respecting vessels employed in smuggling considerable quantities of salt, soap and tobacco from Ireland ... You [are] to consider and submit to the Board such measures as you may deem will be most effectual for putting a stop thereto, keeping it always in view that the benefit or advantage to the revenue that may reasonably be expected to arise from the adoption of any such measures must be such as to counterbalance any expense which may attend the carrying them into execution.' Their reply has not been traced.

The European East India markets also supplied their goods direct.

Holland

On 30 September 1788 the Board wrote 'It appears that it is become almost a general practice for ships from Holland and the east countries to bring in clandestinely considerable quantities of spirits over and above the allowance for stores, also tea and other dry goods, the spirits in stone bottles and the dry goods in small packages such as paper parcels etc for the better conveniency of private stowage, which goods are secreted in the men's chests and bedding, in the ballast and in private concealments about the ships. And when discovered the plea of the masters is that they were brought on board privately and concealed by the crew without their knowledge and contrary to their orders ...'

This is one of the earliest references to independent smuggles. But full cargoes were also smuggled. In November 1789 'The commissioners having received information that a vessel sailed from Ostend for the west of Scotland about the 23rd of last month loaded with tea, rum, brandy, gin and tobacco. That she is full loaded, part of her cargo for Dumfries and from thence to the westward. That she is a sloop rigged in the form of a smack with a running bowsprit and a short slack topmast and that she is able to carry 800 barrels. That she was formerly one of His Majesty's packets from Dover with the Flemish and French mails and that she sails round the south of England at this time for the west coast of Scotland.'

Gothenburg

On 20 October 1750 George Moore wrote to 'Sir' in Kirkcudbright 'Captain Wilson from Gothenburg arrived here yesterday and this evening that part of his cargo destined here was discharged, consisting of fifty-four chests and boxes of merchandise, which are lodged with me for the owner's account. You are no doubt acquainted that our collector requires the view of the original invoice and sworn to before he grants an invoice for the above merchandise, which pay duty according to value.'

In March 1783 Armstrong at Newcastle reported to the Board in London 'that for the last twelve months I have received frequent intelligence of a smuggling trade carrying on from Gothenburg into the west coast of Scotland with an armed force. And particularly on the 9th and 10th of December last, when a very large quantity of tea and other goods were landed in Galloway in Scotland out of an armed lugger and the 28th ult an armed cutter of twenty-two six and nine pounders landed in the same place 600 ankers of spirits and 300 boxes of tea ... purchased by the smugglers at Langholm in Scotland and the borders thereof, who have associated themselves into formidable bodies to carry and convey these goods through the country into Cumberland, Northumberland, Newcastle and the Southern Counties with firearms, threatening the riding officers in this port with murder whenever they meet them.'

Europe also supplied her own goods to the smugglers.

Malaga

On 5 October 1791 Mr Mark Gregory, consul at Malaga, signified to the Board, in consequence of commands from His Majesty's Principal Secretary of State for foreign affairs that 'the sloop *Nell*, Alex Caithness master, burthen 60 tons sailed from Malaga on the 23 September last for your port [Dumfries] laden with six butts wine all intended to be landed at your port. I am directed to acquaint you that when the vessel arrives you are to report how far the same agrees with the quantity entered ...'

The next two chapters deal with the preventive officers at the receiving end of all these forewarnings.

CHAPTER FIVE: THE PREVENTIVES AT SEA

'Were the importations to the extent stated in the information we can scarcely think that would escape Captain McConnochie and his crew, who we have no reason to doubt but keeps a smart look out and is as much at sea as the size and accommodation of his boat will admit. But it is now nearly twelve months since he brought any of them in. During the spring and summer 1795 he seized three boats, the first of the burthen of 11 tons with about 66 cwt of salt, the second about 17 tons with 112 cwt and the third about 8 tons with 157 cwt salt.' (Collector at Dumfries to the Board, 17 June 1796)

The preventives are all those organisations who were involved at one level or another in attempting to suppress smuggling. These included customs, excise, the navy and the military. This chapter considers the preventives at sea - the king's boats which were attached to the local outports, the excise hulks, the revenue cruisers who covered a wider area, the admiralty vessels who were ordered to patrol the coast until they had to be transferred elsewhere and the coast guard who were appointed in the early 1820s.

The King's Boats
The king's boats were under the charge of the tidesurveyor, referred to as such or as the captain or commander, with four, six or eight boatmen under him. These would appear to have been the obvious answer to the smuggling problem, yet successive colectors had to beg for these boats.

In November 1785 the collector wrote 'Some years ago we gave it as our opinion that the only way we could think of to check or prevent that kind of business [smuggling] upon our part of the coast, which your Honours will recollect extends from the Water of Urr to the Borders of England, was to establish the boat at Carsethorn or Southerness Point, which had been lost with all hands some time before.

'The expense of purchasing such a boat and the pay to the hands must no doubt have been certain and pretty considerable annually and your Honours did not think it advisable to adopt our opinion, especially as the former boat had not made seizures to any considerable extent. But if your Honours are pleased to take a review of the matter and to consider that we have not a boat to board either foreign or coasting vessels in a large tract of coast and that even the preventing of illicit abuses (though no great seizures are made) is of much consequence. We think it probable your Honours would see the matter in the same light we do.

'We have no other view in representing this than the good of the revenue and should it now have your Honours approbation in consequence thereof a good stout boat be appointed with a master and four or five hands, all being thoroughbred sailors, we are humbly of opinion they would either make seizures or prevent smuggling in a great degree on this part of the coast and Firth.'

The King's Boat at Seafield

On 12 January 1743 the boatmen attached to the king's boat at Seafield were deforced 'and miserably beat and wounded.' The surgeon's bill amounted to £4 17s 4d. As the arms belonging to the boat had been taken away by the deforcers, Thomas Bell, the commander, was to list what was needed - and at what price.

After an examination into his conduct, following a complaint by the two surveyor generals, William Craik and David Douglas, Thomas Bell was dismissed in July 1764. He was replaced by Patrick Houston.

In September 1764 Patrick Houston, Thomas Corbet, riding officer, and two tidesman were deforced 'when attempting to destroy five Isle of Man boats. You are to acquaint the said officers that ... had they been obstructed in seizing the boats or in disabling them in such manner as to secure the seizure, the deforcers would in that case [have] incurred the pains of the law. But that the destroying the boats being an illegal act the obstruction they met with therein does not fall within any statute that can inflict punishment on the offenders.

'PS The Board are surprised the said officers with so strong a party did not search for and endeavour to find the goods or a part thereof which had been run out of the boats abovementioned.'

The next month the Board were told that the boat was too small and sharp-built to be of great use, particularly in the winter. The collector made several alternative suggestions. But on 22 December 1766 the Board wrote 'It appearing to us to be now unnecessary to continue the commander and boatmen of the king's boat stationed at Seafield, you are immediately to recall their deputations respectively and transmit the same to us to be cancelled. The boat with her arms, furniture etc are to be brought to Dumfries and there laid up till further orders ...'

The King's Boat at Carsethorn

A chapter in 'Family Histories in Scottish Customs Records' is dedicated to the king's boat at Carsethorn from 1764 to 1792. This looks at the individuals who acted as crew. Here the approach is different as the king's boat is discussed in terms of their impact, or otherwise, on the smuggling.

On 23 July 1782 the king's boat was lost and the four boatmen on board were drowned. 'It appearing by the report of the proper officer from the journal of Mr William Gracie ... that there has been hardly any other service performed by the said boat for five years last passed than the boarding of a few coasters and now and then a ship from foreign parts. And upon the state of the seizures made by the commander and crew ... that the whole amount of the apprized value thereof is only £150 8s 3d, all of which seizures, except one or so, appears to have been made on land without the assistance of the boat. From which it is conceived that the continuing the revenue boat at Dumfries will be an unnecessary expense. You are therefore to report whether any objection occurs to you against discontinuing of the said boat and if you have no objection to offer against that measure you are to report in what measure Mr Gracie ... may be best employed for the benefit of the service till an opportunity shall offer of otherways providing for him. And whether in consequence of not supplying the places of the four deceased boatmen any and what addition to the tidesmen appears indispensibly necessary for the security of the revenue or the better conducting the service.'

In August 1786 a strong case was put forward for the re-establishment of the boat. 'In two or three different letters which we have had occasion to write your Honours on the smuggling business we have given it freely as our opinion that nothing could so effectually check and prevent that trade in this part of the coast as a boat stationed at Carsethorn, manned with eight or ten desperate fellows, who had been aboard a ship of war and accustomed to the sea. Such a boat might cruise from Balcary to Sarkfoot and might board every vessel passing up or down the Firth. Your Honours may easily conceive how difficult a matter it is to convene in a short notice a party of officers scattered at different stations upon a coast of thirty miles in the district of this port ... and even supposing them to be convened how ineffectual must their efforts be in many cases, as they have not only the smugglers but the country to support them. We are aware that it would be attended with considerable annual expense to establish a boat with six or eight men ... but when it is considered that all the carrying business from the places of importation in Galloway is by water in boats of 10 or 15 tons what else but force by water can prevent them? ... We hope your Honours will be so good as forgive the freedom we have taken in stating to your Honours our opinion on the subject. We considered it our duty to do so.'

In 1787 the Rothesay boat was transferred to Carsethorn and in 1788 Robert Carmichael was appointed as the new tidesurveyor. In April the collector sent a letter to the Board. 'We cannot, however, help thinking that your Honours have misapprehended our meaning with regard to an English deputation for Carmichael. Your Honours will be pleased to recollect that from Carsethorn, where he is stationed, he has a view of the English coast and of [the] Solway Firth from off Whitehaven to above Annan. There are no boats stationed upon that part of the coast and ... upon that account only but on account also of the water being much deeper on the English side of the Firth than on this side of it, the smugglers very much prefer going up the Cumberland coast and either smuggling their cargoes there or running them into the Borders. Under these circumstances if Carmichael is limited in his cruises to the Scots coast only the smuggling may be carried on and the smugglers pass under his eye on the opposite side of the Firth to the same extent as ever. And so much were we satisfied of this fact that we charged him to make it his principle care to watch the passages up ... the English channel, as being the most likely track to fall in with the smuggling trade going up to Annan Waterfoot, Sarkfoot or anywhere upon that part of the coast. At the same time he has not to neglect the Scots side of the water towards the Water of Urr. And if in consequence of his being in that track he fell in with the Manx boat the other day and had not Captain Cook just kept in before him he had certainly captured the cutter taken by him and sent into Whitehaven. Both the Manx boat and the cutter taken by Captain Cook were destined for Sarkfoot and both were run ashore on the coast of Cumberland before they were seized. Now had Carmichael in this case been so lucky as to drive both ashore, if a custom house [officer] had come upon him without an English deputation he might have carried away the prizes for which Carmichael had been watching the Firth and lying out in his open boat for four or five nights running. To remedy this inconveniency and to guard against such disappointments it was his wish to have an English deputation and not with a view of departing from his station or of carrying any seizures he might be lucky enough to make to any other port than this. Considering the matter in this point of view and being willing to give every encouragement to Carmichael as a very active officer we cannot help recommending his having an English deputation. And as he promises to sleep very little ashore in the night time we are persuaded he will soon put a stop to smuggling by water in the limits of this port.'

In May 1788 Carmichael wrote to the collector 'representing the smallness of the present boat and praying to be allowed one lately seized by Captain Cook.' The reply from the Board was 'direct Mr Carmichael to use his boat to the best advantage, we being determined not to increase the present establishment.'

A further request was made by the collector in April 1789. 'In our opinion he [Carmichael] will never be able to render any considerable service to the revenue with the present boat because it is impossible he or his crew can remain in the track where smuggling vessels may be expected to pass for three or four nights or a week's cruise in an open boat, constantly wet and having no convenience even to prepare their provisions. Under these circumstances we submit it to your Honours whether it would not be proper to furnish Mr Carmichael with a decked cutter, of 15 or 20 tons burthen, with which he could lay out for a week together. The cost we suppose would not exceed £50 or £60 and perhaps an additional hand or two which would not increase very much the establishment and which we think inadequate at present to the purpose. We understand there is a very clever cutter of the description we have recommended for sale just now in the Cumberland coast. If your Honours approve we shall make further enquiry about her and report.' The proposal was not accepted.

Carmichael was dismissed in 1791, for collusion with the smugglers (Robert McDowall, who acted as a character witness, is discussed in Chapter Eight).

A new appointment was made as part of a joint plan put forward in January 1792 by the Boards of Customs and Excise. One of the customs aims was to provide 'A fitter boat than the present one to be stationed at Carsethorn and two additional boatmen ...' They were able to report that they had 'also purchased a new boat for the station at Carsethorn and appointed Mr Hugh McConnochie commander.' McConnochie had been mate of the *Prince Augustus Frederick* cutter stationed at Ayr.

On 31 January 1792 McConnochie made a request for arms for the boat: eight musquets with bayonets; eight cartouch boxes; three cutlasses; two small brass blunderbusses and one large brass blunderbus on a swivel. 'And as Mr McConnochie may frequently have occasion to be at Whitehaven in the execution of his duty he is to provide for the use of the said boat upon the best and cheapest terms 14 lbs of gunpowder, 28 lbs of ball for the muskets and 20 lbs of ball for the three blunderbusses ...'

Despite all their earlier hopes, there were not many seizures, as can be seen from the table reproduced in the letter-book dated 16 February 1805.

On 2 April 1799 the Board wrote 'It appearing that from the present state of smuggling the boat under the command of Mr McConnochie at Carsethorn is useless to the revenue, the Board appoint Mr McConnochie to be second mate of the *Royal George* cutter ... And the Board direct that from and after the 3rd inst the said boat be laid aside and the crew dismissed, but as tidesmen are wanted at Port Glasgow the

Board will upon their application and upon proper account of their being fit and qualified for the duties of tidesmen appoint them accordingly.'

Table showing the King's Boat at Carsethorn's Seizures 1792-1799

Return of Seizure Date	No. of Boats	Names of Seizure Makers
26 April 1792	Two	Hugh McConnochie, Andrew Taylor, John Lawson, Robert Ostle, Mungo Robb, Samuel Lowdon, James Irving, David Bewley and John Coupland
18 February 1795	One	Hugh McConnochie, Andrew Taylor, John Lawson, Robert Ostle, Samuel Lowdon, David Bewley, John Coupland and Robert Shannon
23 June 1795	One	as above
20 July 1795	One	as above
24 August 1797	One	Hugh McConnochie, Andrew Taylor, John Lawson, Robert Ostle, Samuel Lowdon, David Bewley, and John Coupland

This was not the end of requests for a boat at Carsethorn. On 26 March 1816 the collector wrote 'we therefore beg leave to suggest that a preventive boat be stationed at Carsethorn to scour the coast from the Urr to Sarkfoot. And which we are persuaded would be of great service when acting in co-operation with those stationed on the Cumberland coast.'

Freelancers

In July 1743 the Board agreed to the proposal from Charles Blair, tidesman at Colvend, that 'if he had a boat he is confident he could make a good many seizures, as the boats from the Isle of Man for most part anchor near his station during the ebb tide. And if he was allowed the use of a boat seized by Thomas Bell and now condemned, he proposes to pay the boatmen he is to employ.' This was provided the revenue was put to no expense.

The venture was not successful. On 11 January 1744 the collector acquainted the Board that Blair 'desires the boat may be taken off his hands'. The Board commented 'as she was purchased at the request and upon the proposal of Charles Blair and the revenue was to be at no expense beyond the first purchase ... We are surprised at his not abiding thereby and you are to leave the boat to his disposal and to deduct from his salary the sum paid for the boat and to let us know when you have so done.'

The Hulks

The hulks were old vessels run ashore and used as accommodation for excise officers. The *Justice* hulk at Drummore, and its commander Hugh Stewart, appear frequently in the Stranraer letter-books between 1789 and 1799.

In November 1789 Stewart seized a boat with ten bags of salt at Port Nessock and the Board directed that this should be condemned before the Justices of the Peace. But the collector reported on 25 November that the boat had been 'burnt without that order being carried into execution by Mr McIntyre, while in a state of intoxication, who acted as commander of the *Justice* hulk during the absence of Mr Stewart upon leave. And upon considering the enquiry made into this affair by Mr Oliphant, tidesurveyor, in consequence of your order, we acquaint you that it was your business ... to have sent for Mr Stewart for information from him of the merits of the seizure and being satisfied therewith then to have proceeded yourselves to the condemnation thereof before the justices and not to have left that matter to Mr Stewart, as it appears by your letter you did. And in the meantime you ought to have given proper directions to Mr Stewart for scuttling and securing the boat till condemnation, which would have prevented all the mischief that has happened. When you heard of what had happened instead of sending to an inferior officer to make the enquiry it was the business of the collector to have proceeded himself and enquired into the same ... and the collector is to account for not having done so.

'It appearing from Mr Oliphant's report that one of the crew of the hulk was absent with Mr Stewart ... we direct you to call on Mr Stewart to report in what capacity the man who was absent acts and you are to acquaint Mr Stewart that he has no power whatever to grant any person leave, and that he is not to take upon him to do so in future.'

On 4 December 1789 the collector justified his actions 'in which letter you observe that the crew of the *Justice* hulk do not by any means think themselves subordinate to you and that the step taken by Mr McIntyre was in mere contempt of your authority. We direct you to acquaint the commander and crew that they are under your immediate direction and that they are to consult and advise with you upon every occasion and to follow instructions and orders as you shall think it proper to give them for the good of the service.'

In June 1790 Stewart was concerned about the removal of the military from the district and requested two additional crew. 'And that the security of the hulk, which you [the collector] conceive to be in danger of being destroyed by the smugglers, induce you to think that the party on board of her should be augmented ...' Stewart was not to absent himself from hulk during absence of military 'either by day or by night and that he do also keep the men presently belonging to her constantly on duty on board to prevent any incident to the hulk'.

A letter of the same date requested three weeks leace of absence for William McNish, tidesurveyor, 'to attend to his private affairs ... which you state you are of opinion may be granted without risk of injury to the revenue. And we acquaint you that it was very improper in you to apply for leave for the surveyor and to state that you know no particular duty that will require his attendance at the port absolutely necessary when you were by the same post telling us that there was a certainty of a fraud being attempted within the hulk's district in the absence of the military and proposing to load the revenue with additional expense.

'We therefore not only refuse the request but admonish you to be more consistent and attentive to the security of the revenue in future and we also direct that you as well as the surveyor and all the other officers in the district ...'

When the collector submitted the list of established and incidental officers in August 1790, the Board commented 'and it appears therefrom that Alexander McKie mariner on board the hulk has been discharged without our knowledge. We direct you to charge Mr Stewart ... for having discharged the said Alexander McKie and entering another man in his room without consulting us and without receiving our permission. Request his answer directly in writing.'

The *Justice* hulk was given up in December 1798 and in 1799 the Board commented on the refusal of various members of the crew - George Stewart, John McCane and Thomas Bell, to be transferred to Greenock. The first two resigned rather than 'proceed to Greenock' while Bell's salary was discontinued and his deputation cancelled.

Revenue Cutters

On 13 September 1802 the Board instructed the collector 'in all cases where you receive information of a smuggling vessel being within the limits of your port you transmit by post the earliest account of such intelligence to the commanders of the cutters on the west coast (for which purpose a note of their stations and addresses is subjoined) in addition to the advice you send to the neighbouring ports ...

Royal George cutter, Captain Crawford, station Cumbraes. Letters sent to Port Glasgow. This cutter has been sold and a new one is at present building.
Prince William Henry, Captain Hamilton, station Lamlash and Arran. Letters addressed Irvine by Saltcoats.
Prince Edward, Sir John Reid Bart, station Isle of Whithorn. Letters addressed Isle of Whithorn.
Prince of Wales, Captain Campbell, station Islay. Letters addressed Islay by Tarbert.
Prince Ernest Augustus, Captain Reid, station Stornoway. Letters addressed Stornoway.
Prince Augustus Frederick, Messrs McNeight and Davie, station Ayr. Letters addressed Ayr.

In February 1810 the Board having received information that smuggling 'to a considerable extent is carried on between Girvan and

Stranraer have resolved that the *Royal George* and *Prince of Wales* cutters shall cruise in concert off that part of the coast for the protection thereof and to suppress illegal trade under your orders. And have directed that the cutters proceed to Stranraer accordingly, the *Prince of Wales* immediately and the *Royal George* as soon as she is ready for sea, being at present refitting. You will therefore on the arrival of the cutters respectively give such orders and instructions for executing the service in question as your local knowledge, experience and information shall suggest as proper to be followed, taking care in particular that the cutters be actively employed and that the commanders frequently communicate with Messrs Jeffrey and Eaton, the riding officers on shore, between all of whom a joint plan of operations should be formed. You will report the proceedings of cutters and riding officers with the reult to the Board from time to time.'

The collector's response can be reconstructed, 'stating that according to your information there has been no smuggling to any extent between those places for several months past and that it is much more extensively carried on between Loch Ryan and the Mull of Galloway, particularly to the southward of Port Patrick. And observing that you have no reason to believe that Mr Eaton, since he was stationed at Port Nessock, has added much to the protection of the revenue and that he wants local knowledge.

'I have it in command to acquaint you that the commanders of the said cutters have been directed to extend their cruise from Girvan to the Mull of Galloway, rendezvousing in Loch Ryan in order to communicate with you and the preventive officers. And you are to issue such orders to the commanders from time to time as shall appear to you most proper for the interest of the revenue in directing their attention to any particular part of the coast within the said limits ...'

Coast Guard

The coast guard was established in this area in 1821 and the collectors were required to consider whether or not this would lead to a reduction in their customs establishment. The collector wrote on 27 December 1821 'We are of opinion no reduction can take place in the numbers of officers and clerks at this port consistent with the good of the service and a due and proper regard to the prevention of smuggling. That the tidesmen at their respective creeks act as tidewaiters. Should the preventive waterguard lately established at Southerness continue on a permanent footing, it may perhaps be advisable hereafter to dispense with the services of John Martin tidesman at Carsethorn and also of William Anderson tidesmen at New Abbey and William Hyslop tidesman at Ruthwell. But till a longer trial has fully proved the use of it we have not thought it proper to recommend any reduction for the present.'

The following coast guard boats were established in the Dumfries and Wigtown areas:

      Two at Southerness, Port of Dumfries
      Two at Balcary, Port of Kirkcudbright
      Two at Balmangan, Port of Kirkcudbright
      One at Port William, Port of Wigtown

No equivalent listing has been found for the Port of Stranraer.

In 1822 there were long negotiations with Mr R A Oswald proprietor of the land at Southerness where it was proposed to erect suitable buildings for the coast guard. He wrote on 14 May 1822 'I have today heard ... that Mr Monteath is willing to resign his lease of the building called the Hotel there. By his lease which expires at Whitsunday 1823, he pays me £20 of annual rent and in the course of his lease, which was for twelve years, he came bound to expend £200 on some additional buildings, which have been erected and which sum he was to be repaid at the expiry of his lease ... The sum which will fall to be repaid by him is about £150 at this term. If the premises will suit the purpose intended by the Board and they chose to take them, I am willing to let them for such term as they may chose on their paying me £150 at the term of their entry and an annual rent of £25 during their occupation, payable in equal portion at Whitsunday and Martinmas yearly. And for any ground which they may wish to occupy along with them the yearly rent of £1 a year per acre or in proportion, they to enclose the same at their expense and keep up the enclosures. Should these buildings not suit the purposes of the Board and they should chose to build on the adjacent period I shall require a rent of £2 per acre, they to enclose the same in a similar manner. If they take the buildings as they now stand, the fixtures and such furniture as is in them and to which I have right may be taken at appraisement or sold before they take possession ... I shall condition that in case they take them they shall be left in a state of repair similar to which they shall receive them - or if they shall build that the ground shall be restored ... if from any change of plan the Board shall not use them for the purposes required, they being at liberty to remove any creation they may have made. But that they shall have no power in either to lose, to let or sell the buildings for any other purpose whatever ...'

The Inspecting Commander, Thomas Lavin, wrote on 20 May 1822 'though I have never seen the interior yet I have no doubt but it might be made to accommodate four families and the out building be made into two dwellings, which is all that would be wanted for the crew ... [who] might at once be accommodated with lodgings and perhaps at as little expense to the government as building new houses ...'

On 11 June 1823 the coast guard at Southerness seized 29 lbs of tea, which had to be restored once it was proved that the duty had been paid. The coast guard was withdrawn from here in December 1823.

Navy

The admiralty vessels, when not engaged elsewhere, were expected to cruise along the coasts to suppress smuggling. But when there were problems of national significance then the situation was reversed and the revenue cutters were expected to assist them.

In October 1783 the collector at Whitehaven suggested 'if two or three stout admiralty cutters, not less than twenty guns, were stationed on the coast of the Isle of Man and Scotland it might be a means of frustrating the designs of those notorious sets of people which carry on that illicit trade.'

In early November 1803 the collector at Stranraer wrote to the Board about a smuggling lugger in Clanyard Bay 'You having stated in the postscript to your said letter that you would have informed the revenue cruisers but they being under admiralty orders you thought it would be of no service. I have it in command to acquaint you that although the cutters are under the command of the officers of His Majesty's navy there appears no objection to your acquainting the commanders of the cutters with intelligence as to smuggling vessels that they may proceed in quest of such vessels, if authorised so to do by the officers of His Majesty's navy under whose command they are ...'

This was confirmed in a letter from Captain Sandford Tatham, regulating officer at Greenock, who stated that 'whenever it is certified to him that there is any vessel on the coast committing frauds on the revenue he will immediately attend thereto and direct a cutter or cutters as circumstances require and the service will admit to proceed accordingly. But in selecting for this or any other service it is his wish to apportion the duty as equally as possible that there may be no cause for murmuring on that head.'

In October 1801 Lieutenant Lawd, commander of the armed brig *Laurel*, reported having 'fallen in with a small sloop called the *Peggy* of Belfast, having no register nor dispatches on board, which he brought into Stranraer upon suspicion that she was to be illegally employed and delivered [her] to your charge ...' Lawd requested from the Board deputations for himself and Mr Yawkins, his sailing master, to seize uncustomed goods. But according to the Act 26 Geo 3 Cap 40 Sec 27 officers of the navy already had these powers.

Deputations

Because of its location in the Irish sea (see Figure 2), other countries wanted deputations to seize goods in Dumfries and Galloway while the commanders of the king's boats in turn wanted deputations to seize in England (see section on the king's boats). Some of those who were granted deputatiosn by Edinburgh are listed below:

English Revenue
1778: John Mill, mate of the *Hussar* cruising vessel
Irish Revenue
1789: Edmond McNeil, commander if the revenue barge in Larne
1790: Alexander Hamilton, commander of the *Winder* revenue cruiser
1790: Thomas Hampton, commander of the *Hutchinson* cruising barge.

The following letters come from the Whitehaven letter-books. They are addressed from the Board in London to the collector.

19 January 1754: 'The commissioners of the customs at Edinburgh having by their letter of the 10th inst signified to us that Mr George Dow, commander of the *Sincerity* cruiser at your port and who has a deputation from the Board, having complained that a boat from the Isleman lately seized and carried to Kirkcudbright was stolen by the drunkenness and conniving of James Gordon mate of the *Sincerity*. They directed the collector and comptroller of Kirkcudbright to enquire into the said complaint, who have acquainted them that they required Mr Dow to be present at the examination and to bring such evidences as he thought proper in support of the charge. But that he did not attend. And that it appears by the declaration of six of the crew of the *Sincerity* cruiser, who were in the barge belonging to the cruiser at the seizing and securing the boat, that they were not allowed to attend in order to be examined and that it likewise appears by the examinations of several persons on oath ... that the boat was carried off while the mate was lodging the goods in the king's warehouse and that during that time Mr Dow was in a public house near the shore where the boat lay in company with - Johnston, master of the said boat. We direct you to make strict enquiry into this affair with respect to the said Dow and charge him therewith, take his answer in writing and transmit both charge and answer to us with your observations and opinions ...'

16 February 1754: 'We received your letter of the 6th instant with the charge and answer of Captain Dow ... and considered the same together with your observations thereon we direct you to reprimand Captain Dow, it appearing to us that through his great negligence the ... boat was suffered to be taken away by the smugglers, that he had not given orders for scuttling her, as alleged by him, and that he prevented several of his crew at Kirkcudbright and likewise at your port from giving their attendance, as required by the respective collectors in order to their being properly examined ... and letting him know that if he is culpable in the like manner we shall take other measures for the service.'

The next chapter considers the preventives on land.

CHAPTER SIX: THE PREVENTIVES ON LAND

'The Board having taken into consideration the alarming state of smuggling on the west coast of Scotland, particularly in the Bay of Luce, and [being] desirous of adopting in concert with the Commissioners of Excise such measures as might give effectual check to this pernicious traffic they communicated their sentiments thereon to the Board and the same having been maturely considered I have it in command to signify to you the general plan agreed to be carried into execution being the result of joint deliberations of both Boards upon this important subject that you may the better further the interest of the revenue. Viz:

'The Commissioners of Excise agreed to make the following appointments at the sole expense of the revenue. A riding officer to be stationed at Gatehouse, to patrol the roads with the military. Another at Gretna Green and a third at Glenluce. These persons and the riding officer at Stewarton, who will be afterwards taken notice of, are to meet to carry intelligence to one another daily, to co-operate with one another and use their best endeavours to prevent or detect the pernicious practice of smuggling upon the coasts in the neighbourhood of their respective stations ...

'The Board of Customs on their part determined to make the following arrangements and appointments under their directions only at their expense. The barrack at Port William to be continued but instead of the former number of officers in it there is to be a new commander with a preventive officer in addition to the present tidesman. A riding officer to be stationed at Newton Stewart, lying betwixt Gatehouse and Glenluce ...

'I have it further in command to enjoin you and the several officers under your survey to exert your best endeavours upon this occasion so as to defeat the smugglers in their plans and operations and to advise the Board from time to time of your proceedings, taking care that the greatest harmony be kept up with the officers under the Board of Excise.' (Board to the collector at Dumfries 24 January 1792).

The preventives on land were the customs, excise and the military.

The Customs

Frequent references have been made throughout this book to various grades of customs officers. As the establishment varied from outport to outport and from one period to the next, it is difficult to give firm definitions of exactly what was involved in each officer's post. The following family tree is intended to provide a general picture.

Collector: in overall charge of the outport and directly responsible to the Board. Several of the longer and more detailed letters quoted from 1780 onwards were written by David Staig of Dumfries.

Comptroller: the financial manager and second in command to the collector

Surveyor general: in overall charge of the other officers along the coast (often called a landsurveyor). Throughout most of the period studied there were two surveyors general at Dumfries, William Craik to the west and David Douglas to the west.

Tidesurveyor: responsible for rummaging the vessels anchored in the port. He also commanded the king's boat, if one existed.

Riding officer: with approximately ten miles of coast to cover, in theory on horseback, in search of smugglers

Landwaiter: in charge of supervising the unloading of the cargoes of vessels from foreign ports. He was supposed to record the cargo in the 'blue book'. He also attended the shipping of goods. Not all ships arriving at/departing from the port could be attended by the landwaiter so that he was either assisted by the surveyor or delegated to the tidesmen

Tidesman: responsible for coastwise shipping at a creek and also used for quarantine duty and looking out for smugglers. Often the post is synonymous with tidewaiter. The creeks where the tidesmen were stationed in the Dumfries district included Annan, Carsethorn,

Cummertrees Powfoot, Dornock, Glencaple, Kelton, New Abbey, Ruthwell and Southerness.

Boatman: attached to the king's boat.

These job descriptions were not hard and fast - the men combined forces, particularly over smuggling. Any seizure might be made by the collector, surveyor general, riding officer and three tidesmen or by a tidesman on his own.

The officers did not lead easy lives. As has been seen already the 'country' was against them, when they made a seizure they were deforced and even after the goods were in the king's warehouse they were not necessarily safe.

The collector reported to the Board on 24 April 1724 'I have been at Kirkcudbright and have made what trial there I can about the deforcement of the officers, breaking open the warehouse and carrying off the goods seized by Mr Douglas. And also about the owners and proprietors of these goods. But have not had same good success therein as I could have wished, though I did all that lay in my power.

'I examined Samuel Graham, boatman, and Duncan Ferguson, extra tidesman, who were upon the watch when the warehouse was broken, upon oath. And they are very express as to several women and one man ... but they are all servants and of little account. However, the punishment of them effectually will deter others from like practices in time to come. I used all possible means with several other persons, who I suspected knew something of that affair, to make a discovery thereof but could not prevail with any of them either by fair means or foul. However I have annexed a list [not transcribed] of several persons who I am confident were accessory to that deforcement that your Honours may if you think fit prosecute some of them and reserve the rest for evidences. I wrote to Mr Hamilton to take the oaths of the three boatmen at this port, who were upon the watch with our officers ... but as they were entire strangers at Kirkcudbright their evidence is of no account.

'I could not by any means get proof of the owners of the goods. They are generally believed to belong to Baillie David McClelland and Alexander Hesker, merchant in Kirkcudbright ... Fisher, the master of the ship, would on no account make any discovery to me. He owns that he was employed to go to the Island [Isle of Man] for four hogsheads of wine but denies that he knew anything of rum, brandy or tobacco being put on board his ship. He is no doubt taught this by his freighters and by them still kept in hopes of getting back his ship. But I am confident when it comes to the extremity and his ship legally condemned he will make a discovery of the owners of these goods. Unless they pay him all damages which he hath sustained, which I do not think they are well able to do ...

'I was informed at Kirkcudbright that there had been an arrestment laid upon the ship in that river by William Dunbar, messenger, by virtue of an admiral precipe, as he alleged, at the instance of one John McClelland, a carrier in that town, some days before the goods were discharged. I sent for Dunbar ... but [he] would not show it [the assistance] me pretending he had given it back to McClelland, who employed him. And McLelland was either gone out of town or kept himself out of the way so that I could not find him. But I have written to Mr Douglas to send me the copy of the arrestment which he received from the messenger ...'

'As the owners of these goods have certainly been advised to take these measures by some officious person, I humbly conceive it might be of some service in this affair to call both Dunbar and McClelland to an account for laying on this arrestment. For I am persuaded there was no foundation for it but was done merely to frighten and hinder Mr Douglas from carrying that ship out of the river to some port where he might have secured the goods. And I don't see but they are liable in the damages that have ensued to the king and seizure makers upon this arrestment.'

Sometimes there were clashes between fellow officers. In December 1782 David Douglas, surveyor general, and George Halliday, tidesman, seized two Manx boats. The story continued as follows:

March 1784: the Board's solicitor sent a writ of delievry from the Exchequer directing 'that the hulls of two Manx boats seized by Mr

Douglas to be broken up and thereafter the materials with the furniture and apparel of said boats to be sold'. The collector reported 'We put the writ into Mr Douglas's hands for that purpose and he returned us the certificate ... signed by Andrew Smith, tidesman, and John Beattie, who wrote by his own hand, and dated 6th April, declaring they were broken up and destroyed accordingly.'
April 1784: 'Having made the necessary intimation, we proceeded to dispose of the materials and furniture the 7th April and having exposed them at £4 they were sold at £4 5s ... John Martin was the purchaser. But Mr Douglas paid us the price and at that time we had no other idea than that the boats were a heap of rubbish fit for firewood only. It turns out however that they had been very superficially broken up or undergone some repair for Mr Douglas admits that he sold one of them thereafter for £10 and the other he gave away to the Captain of the *Pigmy* [his son]. But Mr Douglas had not our approbation to the measure nor did he communicate any such design or intention to us ... We shall only further observe as the boats were lying nigh Annan, eighteen or nineteen miles from this place, and as the writ was directed to Mr Douglas as well as us we did not think it absolutely necessary for us to go that length upon the business since he was residing within a few miles of the spot.

May 1785: George Halliday claimed his share of the two boats, offering to establish his right by the evidence of Andrew Smith and his own oath.

June 1785: The collector wrote to George Halliday 'We desire to know from you whether you saw these boats after the 6th of April [1784], when they were certified to be broken up. And you are to report on what condition they were and in short every circumstance you know with regard to the disposal of them. You are also desired to acquaint us in what manner you mean to establish your right to a share of the produce of these boats and by what evidence you can establish that you were present and assisting at the seizing of them. And it will be highly necessary that you be recollected with respect to all these particulars as it is probable you will be called to declare them upon oath.'

Halliday was summoned to attend to the custom house on Thursday, 28 June 1785 but did not appear. The collector sent a further letter two days later. 'We ... send down Baldwin Martin to take charge of your duty till you return and we desire you to come here without loss of time.'

January 1787: a second certificate of sale and expenses was produced. Halliday received his share.

The Excise

Despite the exhortations of both Boards, the customs and excise did not always work well together. The following story comes from the Port Glasgow and Greenock letter-books.

In January 1765 'In obedience to the reference on the enclosed from the collector and comptroller of Port Patrick and John McWilliam, officer of excise there, in relation to a seizure of foreign spirits brought in here the 4th December last by Martin Campbell, mate of the *Prince of Wales* wherry and Samuel McQuirk commander of the *Boscawen* wherry, employed by Captains Barker and Gellie, being part of return No 1203 and the same condemned in the Court of Exchequer last term, we beg leave to acquaint that we called on said Martin Campbell and on Archibald Thomson, mate of the *Boscawen* wherry, who happened to command her when that seizure was made, and caused each of them to give a declaration in writing of the facts and circumstances which attended that affair, which with the declaration of Thomas Ryan, sailor on board the *Boscawen* and John Campbell and Archibald Stewart, belonging to the *Prince of Wales* wherry ... they represent that in the month of November last ... Martin Campbell and Samuel McQuirk, having made a concert to assist each other, upon an information of sundry boats with spirits being expected from the Isle of Man and that on the 28th [November] ... early in the morning they fell in with three Manx boats loaded off Girvan, one of which was seized by the *Boscawen* wherry. The other two made off alongst the coast towards the Isle of Man, on which both the *Prince of Wales* and *Boscawen* wherries followed them till after mid day often firing at them, which alarmed the people on the coast who saw the chase. That a little to the northward of Port Patrick a shot from the *Boscawen* broke away the fore halyards of the sternmost of the two smuggling boats, on which she run ashore (and the other made her escape). The *Boscawen* wherry, who was nearest, having left her long boat to attend the seizure made that morning, anchored immediately within gunshot of the boat on shore to cover the seizure with her guns from any attempts of the country people, who crowded about. And the *Prince of Wales*, having come up in a short time with a long boat, landed directly to take possession of the seizure. And found the revenue officers from Port Patrick with some military there, who were loading the spirits on board boats they had brought with them from that port on hearing their firing and seeing the chase, which however they took on board their wherries, judging that they had a right to the whole seizure, which they performed without any violence or threatenings, as alleged by Mr McWilliam the excise officer. That at that time neither Mr Fraser nor any other of the Port Patrick officers pretended any right to the seizures in question, which indeed they proposed to have lodged at that port. And that the comptroller only seemed at a loss how he was to be reimbursed in the charges incurred by their having brought boats and a party of soldiers on that occasion, on which they gave them three ankers of the spirits [from] the seizure makers' share which, with some few casks they got on shore, they judged sufficient to indemnify them for that expense. That before they got under sail with the wherries all the people were away from the Manx boat, which was settled a shore on the beach. Consequently had any person been left on board her, he could not perish, as set forth by Mr McWilliam. And that what was lost and taken away of the seizure by the country people was in a great measure owing to the Port Patrick officers interfering and coming in with their boats between the *Boscawen* wherry's guns and the Manx boat and mixing with the mob, which hindered firing to the shore for fear of damage to them, whom they knew to be revenue officers by having the military with them. As to the account of charges laid out by the comptroller of Port Patrick on that affair ... Martin Campbell and his partner can have no objection thereto, as it does not consist with their knowledge what was necessary or actually laid out but presume Mr Fraser has given a true state of it ...'

The argument continued. In June 1765 the collector at Port Glasgow and Greenock wrote to the Board in reply to their letters 'directing us to acquaint Mr Colin Campbell, commander of the *Prince of Wales* wherry and Lieutenants Barker and Gellie that your Honours expected they would at least pursue the contents of your letter of the 20th March last in proportion to the sum retained as their own shares out of the seizure makers' moiety of the goods seized at Port Patrick ... and accordingly pay the money to us to be paid over to Mr James Frazer, deputy comptroller, and Mr John McWilliam, officer of excise. We beg leave to acquaint your Honours that we should have answered ... before now but we could not get Lieutenants Barker and Gellie and Captain Colin Campbell all present at one time in order to get their answers. We have communicated your Honours letter to them separately as they arrived but they would give us no answer until they were all together. This day Lieutenants Barker and Gellie arrived here with the *Cullen* under their command and we have again desired their answer ... and they acquaint us that they will themselves write your Honours a full state of the case but they think the comptroller and excise officer at Stranraer have no right to any part of the seizure made by them off Port Patrick more than they have already got, which they say is the boat and several casks. They also say they are certain the enquiry made by the collector of excise at Dumfries before the magistrates or justices at Stranraer was not fair and candid and only one party present. And they say if the comptroller and officer of excise think they have a right to any more of the seizure they must prove their right before the Barons of Exchequer ...'

On 18 June 1765 the collector replied to the Board's letter 'acquainting us that you expect Mr Colin Campbell will punctually comply with the opinion of the Board in satisfying Mr James Frazer ... and Mr John McWilliam ... in the manner recommended in your Honours letter ... and if Mr Barker and Mr Gellie do not do the same, or give much better reason for not doing it than they have yet done your Honours will think it your duty to support the officers in procuring justice ...

'As Mr Campbell has not been at home for a considerable time past, we cannot get his answer, and we have communicated the above to Messrs Barker and Gellie who acquaint us that they are still unwilling to make any allowance ... but that they will write your Honours a state of the affair with their reasons before they set out for England, which they propose to do in a few days.'

The end of the story has not been traced as yet.

In November 1784 Baldwin Martin, tidesman, was given information by John Walls, an excise officer, that there had been a smuggle at Thornhill. He was paid 11s 10d to cover his costs over this 'false alarm'.

The Military
Throughout the eighteenth century there were frequent requests for assistance from the military.

In March 1816 the collector wrote to the Board 'In addition to this preventive boat [at Carsethorn] we also are of opinion it would be perhaps more advisable to erect small houses for two or three of the tidesmen in high commanding situations (as frequently their places of residence are at some distance from the shore) [rather] than military guard houses which must be built at a considerable expense and probably not answer the intended object so well. With respect to the military themselves however we are of opinion a troop of dragoons should be quartered in this place from which might be detached a subaltern's party to Arran and a sergeant's or corporal's to Carsethorn. For illicit distillation is carried on to a great length in this district and cannot be effectually checked but by the assistance of country, which species of force can move with rapidity and is therefore more able to act with effect on any sudden intelligence or information being received than infantry.'

Sometimes the response was positive. 'And being of opinion that the present state of smuggling on the west coast of Scotland, which by the reports of the officers is carried on in the most daring manner, requires the very best aid of the military and that the same should be promoted by the best encouragement we therefore resolve that the like allowances as are made in England be made to the military (such assistance be specially certified to us) and that in the distribution thereof the following rules be observed ...'

In December 1809 the Board replied to a letter from the collector at Stranraer 'submitting the expediency of having a detachment of military stationed at Sandhouse Bay for the prevention of smuggling and I have it in command to direct you to report whether the detachment of military proposed to be billeted ... could get proper quarters at that place and be properly supplied with provisions and at similar artes at which they are supplied at Ballantrae.'

But co-operation was not always automatic, as can be seen from reading between the lines of this letter, written from the Board to the collector on 2 October 1764. 'In consequence of an application made by us to the Marquis of Lorn, commanding His Majesty's forces in North Britain, there is to be an officer's command of soldiers quartered this winter at Annan. And we recommend it to you and the other [customs] officers in the most earnest manner to exert yourselves with activity and diligence in order to suppress the pernicious practice of smuggling and to maintain by every act of civility a cordial and friendly correspondence with the officers of His Majesty's troops, who will be enjoined to concur with zeal in every measure for promoting His Majesty's service.'

In July 1802 the collector complained to the Board 'On a late occasion, when a smuggling vessel of a considerable force appeared in the limits of this port, the acting comptroller and land surveyor collected a few commissioned officers of the Dumfriesshire regiment of militia and went out, more with a view of preventing than of hopes of making any seizures. And in this expectation the two officers incurred an expense of £4 14s 11d for themselves and the party assisting them, which the Honourable Board were pleased to disallow which they [the officers] thought rather discouraging as the revenue would have received its share had they been successful in making a seizure. And they hope your Honours will upon considering the matter again be disposed to allow that expense to be reimbursed.' Other references to the expense of using the military have been made elsewhere in the book.

As with the navy, the military also had other priorities. On 14 April 1786 the collector reported 'Having an express from Mr David Douglas ... on Wednesday night last, saying that a vessel had arrived in the neighbourhood of Annan, which he suspected had smuggled goods on board, and desiring assistance we immediately dispatched Mr Twaddel, landwaiter, and Baldwin Martin, tidewaiter, but the military having marched from this place to Manchester no assistance of that kind could be procured. Understanding however that the *Pigmy* cutter was in the neighbourhood of Kirkcudbright we sent an express to the collector of the customs there desiring the information might be communicated to the commander of the cutter that he might run his tender up the Firth in pursuit of said vessel. But Mr Twaddel and Martin being now returned from the Border they report the matter to have been a false alarm and have given in an account of expenses incurred amounting with charge of the express to Kirkcudbright to £1 11 6 ...'

Luckily the troops returned because the Board wrote in October 1786 'it appearing by the cantonment of the troops laid before us by his excellency the commander in chief that there is a detachment of one sergeant and twelve privates at Annan, we intend appointing an extraordinary tidesman and to station him at Annan to co-operate with Thomas Geddis, the tidesman stationed about two miles below that place, who with the assistance of the military, we are of opinion, may render good to the revenue ...'

The next chapters consider the smugglers.

CHAPTER SEVEN: SMUGGLERS - THE VESSELS

'The collector and comptroller of Wigtown having ... transmitted ... a letter which they that day received from Mr Daniel Nicol, commander of preventive officers at Port William, stating that at four o'clock that morning the man on lookout saw a lugger standing out from the Mull of Galloway at five o'clock. She again stood in for the Mull but had not been on the east side of the Bay of Luce. That he supposes her to be the same lugger that was there 20th and 21st ult. That at seven o'clock in the morning she stood up the Bay for Drummore with a small smack accompanying her. And that there is also a brig lying off and on between the Big Stair and the Mull, which appears very suspicious. I have it in command to signify the same to you and to direct you to use your utmost endeavours to prevent and detect any fraud that may be attempted by the vessels in question ... (from the Board to the collector at Stranraer, 15 July 1802).

The term smuggler is applied both to the men who smuggled the goods and the vessels that they used to tranpsort these goods. This chapter concentrates on the vessels while the next chapter considers the men. There is a wealth of information about the vessels because whenever one was either expected or sighted letters were sent to the preventive officers along the coast, exhorting them to attempt seize the vessel and also to detect any goods that were smuggled on shore.

A letter from the collector at Dumfries, dated 16 April 1711 informed the Board 'We having advice on Thursday last of two small boats ... hovering on the coast, all the officers was ordered to be upon their guard to prevent the running of any goods and to observe the sands, where they could discover some tracks of horses and men's feet upon the sand. (We) sent one express on Friday morning whereupon immediately we took horse and went down to Reval, a place upon the Borders, where we made search of all suspected places where run goods might be concealed ...'

As any suspicious vessel heading up the Solway had basically nowhere to go but the coast of Dumfries or Cumberland, it was possible to track her movements in detail (see Figure 8). Here is one example.

To Mr David Douglas, Surveyor General, 17 April 1786, 'By express we send you inclosed a copy of a letter [not transcribed in the letter-book] we have just now received from Collector Laurie of Kirkcudbright and have to desire that you will without loss of time follow out the matter in terms of Mr Laurie's letter ...'

The collector at Kirkcudbright had also informed the commander of the *Pigmy* tender (Douglas's son), cruising off the Ross, and he sent his cutter up the Firth.

To Mr Laurie, collector at Kirkcudbright, 18 April 1786, 'Upon receipt of yours of yesterday's date we sent off an express to Mr Douglas and have sent you inclosed a copy of his answer to us by George Halliday tidesman, who will deliver you this and comes to identify the vessel ...'

To Mr David Douglas, 21 April 1786, 'The commander of the *Pigmy* tender having sent up the vessel to Kirkcudbright, which was identified by George Halliday, and she being now in the custody of the collector and comptroller of the customs at that port, it will be necessary you procure every possible information you can as to her discharging her cargo at Browhouses and Lockerfoot, which you will be pleased to forward to us in order that all the vessels and circumstances attending this smuggling adventure may be transmitted to the Board for their consideration ...

'PS Please let us know the names of the persons who can prove the goods were smuggled out of the above vessel.'

To the Board in Edinburgh, 22 April 1786, 'She turning out to be the *Ann and Eliza* of Ayr and not having been at the custom house, we are persuaded she had discharged smuggled goods of some kind. On receiving advice from Mr Laurie that the vessel was in custody we immediately dispatched an express ... this he (Halliday) did without loss of time and knew both vessel and several of the hands ...'

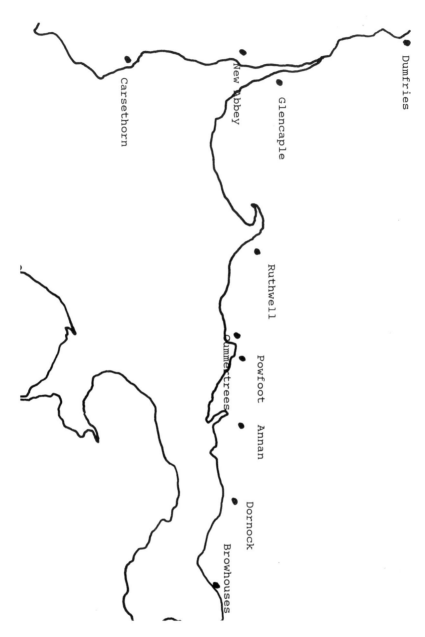

Figure 8: Creeks where Tidesmen were stationed in Dumfries

To Mr Laurie, 23 November 1786, a bill for their costs in attending the seizure, totalling 35s, including 'costs for George Halliday for horse hire expense and trouble going from Annan to Kirkcudbright ...'

To the Board, 24 November 1786, as the collector had been so involved at the correspondence end, was he entitled to a share of the seizure money? The answer from the Board was dated 27 November 'this information having originated with Mr Douglas ... and the vessel seized by Lieutenant Douglas, his son, in consequence thereof. And you having ... been repaid all the expenses in consequence of the said information, including the express to Kirkcudbright, it does not appear that you have any claim upon the seizure. You having done no more than your duty.'

On 25 May 1787 Thomas Geddis sent an express to the collector informing him that a vessel, about 20 tons burthen, had arrived in his district with prohibited goods. The collector instructed the comptroller's clerk, David Douglas, Ebenezer Hepburn, riding officer. Thomas Twaddel, landwaiter, and Joseph Dickson and George Halliday, tidesmen, to go to Dornock, reassuring Geddis in a letter dated 26 May 1787 'herewith [we] send you all assistance in our power. We approve much of your conduct in acquainting us by express and hope you will continue to do so on any future occasion, always describing the vessel and other circumstances as particularly as in your power.'

Despite this, the collector also wrote to Mr Laurie at Kirkcudbright 'but as the vessel will probably be gone before the officers arrive there, we think proper to acquaint you in case Captain Cook be in your harbour or neighbourhood that he may send his tender down the Firth and be upon the lookout if they can catch the vessel upon her return ...'

The report to the Board is dated 28 May 1787. 'Yesterday Mr Hepburn and Mr Twaddel returned and acquainted is that before they got there the goods were all landed and carried off. But the vessel, which Geddis said appeared to him to be the same that he had seen have the goods on board the night before, being still there they went on board of her and having interrogate the master and got no satisfactory account from him they thought themselves justifiable in detaining her and therefore stripped her of her sails etc. She turns out to be a clinker-built cutter, built at Ramsey in the year 1779, registered at Stranraer the 21st March 1787, but has no name upon her except wrote with chalk, the property of Hugh Crane of the parish of Ayr and Daniel Wallace of the parish of Kirkmaiden and county of Wigtown, burthen 15 tons. And had on board six or seven stout sailors with the master. And there being no possibility of getting any person in that country to bring her about, there was two sailors sent from here for that purpose early this morning. And if the weather turn moderate we expect her with the tidesman who was left with the charge of her at Kelton in a few days. When the crew saw the officers were serious in making the vessel a seizure, one of the hands observed that they had no great reason to complain for she had already done enough for her share, or words to that purpose. Indeed we are told that for a considerable time by past either this vessel or some such like has not been less than once a week at the same place always with full cargoes.'

The tidesmen were not always so attentive. On 7 November 1785 the collector wrote to Samuel Wilson, tidesman, 'As we have been credibly informed that one or two smuggling sloops within this month or six weeks have landed in your neighbourhood a large quantity of tobacco, spirits and soap in open day and no officer present. This is therefore to desire you to acquaint us if you know any thing of the matter. And we likeways direct [you] to take all possible pains to find out the names of the vessels, what they were load with and particularly to who the cargoes belonged, and if possible a description of them. This we desire you will take all care to find out and acquaint us with every particular in your power as soon as you can.'

On 5 October 1789 the collector at Kirkcudbright informed Dumfries 'of a vessel which had smuggled her cargo at Balcary being driven on shore at Southwick. Immediately upon receipt of which we sent an express to the officers at Carsethorn [Twaddell and Shaw] but no accounts of any such vessel could be got. We have just now been informed by James Hunter, tidewaiter at Southerness, that on Sunday last a pretty large boat loaded with salt came on shore there, which he went to enquire after. Upon which he was taken prisoner by the crew and detained there till the tide came, when the boat went off again, and we hear she has since landed her cargo in this Firth. Hunter says he read the *Lively* of Kirkcudbright upon her stern and he believes a man of the name of Campbell, who seemed either to be master or owner of her, was on board at the time. Should this vessel return to your port it will therefore be necessary to seize her, for which purpose we give you this information.'

This letter was sent to Mr Carmichael, commander of the king's boat at Carsethorn on 15 December 1794. 'Sir, The last time you was in the custom house we acquainted you that we had been informed of several small boats being up the Border with salt and other such goods and enjoined you to be attentive in your endeavours to prevent such like in time coming. Since which time we understand several such boats have discharged in that quarter, particularly two about ten days ago, one of which after being discharged was seized at Browhouses by Geddis and Brown, tidesmen. We therefore again enjoin you to be particularly attentive in preventing a continuance of such trade. And as Geddis and Brown could not remove the boat, we direct that you do bring the said boat round to Annan Waterfoot or Carsethorn, if she be in a condition to be brought to any of these places.'

This story includes a combination of letters to the Board and various tidesmen along the coast. 'We have this moment received [from the collector and comptroller at Stranraer] advice that a smuggling vessel, cutter-rigged, white sails, black sides ... not mounted with any guns, not a very large vessel and deep laden, was chased off Holyhead by His Majesty's ship *Eling* [Lieutenant Archibold, commander] on the forenoon of the 6th inst but that she made her escape ... standing a north-east course towards the Brough Head.' George Brown, Annan, James Hunter, Carsethorn, William Elliott, Ruthwell and Cummertrees Powfoot, and Thomas Geddis, Dornock, were forewarned of this.

On 11 December 1802 the collector received a joint letter from Geddis and Elliott that the vessel had been in their areas, and discharged goods. At the same time she must have passed Annan and so all three tidesmen were summoned to the custom house the following Tuesday to explain what had happened. In fact neither of the tidesmen had been at their posts and there were 'strong suspicions' that they had both been drinking with the owner of the cargo, Richard Hetherton. Geddis was dismissed and Elliott moved to another station. There is no record of George Brown's excuse.

In 1801 it has been the turn of the collector at Stranraer to be criticised. On 25 January the Board wrote 'Captain Hamilton of *Prince William Henry* cutter having by letter of the 19th inst stated that when he was last in Loch Ryan he heard that a large lugger of eighteen guns and sixty men landed a cargo of brandy and geneva in and about the Bay of Luce. That he spoke a Dundee sloop and that the master thereof said he passed close by her at Port Nessock Bay, near the Mull, and he saw nine or ten ports of a side but no guns run out and mentioned that she appeared to him as long as a frigate. And it appearing by a letter from the collector and comptroller at Wigtown, dated the 23rd current, that on the night of the 8th a lugger smuggled a part of a cargo of spirits and tobacco at the Isle of Killegan, in the west side of the Bay of Luce about thirty miles distant from Port William round the Bay on the opposite side of the Bay of Luce and within the district and only a few miles from Stranraer, I have it in command to acquaint you thereof and to signify that you should have informed the Board of this smuggle and that they expect you will be more attentive in future.'

On 27 February 1805 the collector and comptroller at Carlisle reported that on the previous Friday and Saturday a smuggling vessel had landed part of her cargo near Silloth Bay and that the remainder of the cargo was intended to be smuggled somewhere in the Dumfries precinct. This information was transmitted to the surveyor and all the tidesmen at the creeks. A further letter was sent from Carlisle, dated 22 April, that the same vessel was in the Solway Firth with a cargo of salt 'which is intended to be smuggled upon either the English or Scotch side of the Firth.' Two days later Dumfries informed Kirkcudbright and Sir John Reid, commnader of the *Prince Edward* cutter at Whithorn, 'She is described as being an armed vessel ... about fifteen or sixteen men on board with swivel guns and small guns. We have considered it for the advantage of the revenue to make this communication. Robert Patty is master and owner of this vessel and is a native of the Borders and an old offender.' But, as reported to Carlisle, 'we have not heard that any of the officers have been successful in falling in with the vessel or any part of her cargo, except a few casks that was seized by the officers at the port of Kirkcudbright. We beg leave to return you our thanks for the early information of the fraud intended and should any success attend your present notice we will take the earliest opportunity to acquaint you thereof.'

The co-operation was not always so heartfelt. On 11 July 1820 the collector at Dumfries wrote 'Referring to your Honours order of the 1st June last No 56 directing the *Sarah* of Liverpool to be detained at Annan till further orders, we beg leave to state that we have this morning received a letter from the coastwaiter at Annan, inclosing copy of an order from the Honourable Board of Customs in London to the collector and comptroller of Liverpool and a letter from them, requesting that the *Sarah* may be delivered up to three persons sent from Liverpool to navigate her to that port for the purpose of prosecuting her to condemnation. We beg leave to transmit their documents and to add that we have sent directions to the coastwaiter at Annan to allow the vessel to be taken into deep water but not to deliver her up without authority from your Honours.'

In January 1821 the collector replied to a letter from the Board 'relative to a smuggling vessel said to have lately appeared on the coast within or near the limits of this port and to have landed a considerable quantity of goods ... no smuggling vessel had been within the limits of this port for a considerable term of years. And after the minutest enquiry and the report of the surveyor we think the vessel alluded to must have been the smuggling vessel reported about three months since to have been in Silloth Bay on the coast of Cumberland and there to have affected a landing of brandy and gin, which in a great measure they were said to have been robbed of by the country people. We strongly suspect this to be the same vessel that was reported to us at the time by the collector and comptroller of Carlisle and information which we lost no time in communicating to Sir John Reid, [the] collector and comptroller of Kirkcudbright and to all the waterside officers of this port enjoining the utmost vigilance on their part. About a fortnight after this is was rumoured here that some gin was landed about Browhouses below Annan. The surveyor went to Annan to learn if there was any truth in the report and found that the same rumour prevailed there. That George

Brown, tidesman, and an officer of excise had made diligent search for the same two days before and found nothing. And a subsequent search has been made by several excise officers in the interior, who found nothing except about half a gallon of gin supposed to be from the vessel alluded to, contained in an earthen jar. We beg leave to add it is our opinion and that of the surveyor and other officers consulted that no direct landing has been made in this port or if any it must have been very inconsiderable.'

There follow several examples of the chase and/or seizure of named vessels.

The *Betsey* of Guernsey

In May 1791 the collector reported to the Board 'On the morning of Friday the 13th current betwixt two and three o'clock the collector received a letter from Mr Carmichael, tidesurveyor, advising of his having followed a brig up towards Annan, which proved to be a smuggler, and requesting that a party of dragoons might be immediately sent him. In consequence of which the collector immediately made an application to the commanding officer of the 3rd regiment of dragoons quartered here and a party of thirty-three men was granted and dispatched as soon as possible, alongst with Messrs Shaw and McCornock. A great deal of time had however been delayed on the road by the express and before the party got to Battlehill, the place appointed, the tide was flowed and the vessel was gone about an hour or better. She having discharged her cargo in a few hours after she came aground, previous to the arrival of the dragoons, Mr Carmichael had got fifteen casks of gin and put them on board the king's boat. And upon a further search by Mr Douglas and the other officers, accompanied by the dragoons, they got in different places seven casks of brandy, seven bales tobacco stalks and thirteen bales tobacco, all which is now secured in the king's cellar here, except one cask of brandy that was staved by accident at taking off the cart ...'

On 31 May the collector wrote to the Board 'we have the pleasure to inform your Honours that the smuggling brig is now well secured in the harbour of Whitehaven ...While the search was going on it occurred to Mr McCornock [clerk] as the next step for securing the vessel to return to Annan and by the post then about to leave that place write letters to the collector and comptroller of Whitehaven, Workington, Kirkcudbright and Wigtown and to Captain Cook, informing them of what had passed and describing the vessel in case she should call ... the measure was judicious and succeeded for the vessel made a complete discharge, went into Whitehaven in ballast and was there secured ... The collector and comptroller of Whitehaven, having given us information of that event, we have directed Mr Carmichael with his crew to go over and identify the said vessel, supposing they should be able to do so. It has occurred to us that as the offence was committed in Scotland she might with propriety be seized where she now lies, be brought over to this port and carried into condemnation before the court of exchequer in Scotland should this meet the approbation of your Honours ...' The same day he wrote to Mr Wilson, tidesurveyor at Whitehaven, 'we were in expectation that Mr Carmichael ... would have been with you before this time to identify the vessel you have secured. We have however given him orders to proceed immediately and we hope he will be with you in a day or two. If not write us again and we will endeavour to furnish you with other evidence. But as Carmichael carries with him his boat's crew, all of whom saw the vessel, we can have no doubt they will be able to do the business ...' On 9 June Whitehaven was asked how many hands were on board and whether they had any arms, when the vessel put into their port.

The brigantine *Betsey* was brought back to Carsethorn and on 6 June 1791 she was seized by the collector 'in case the evidence of Mr Carmichael and the boatmen shall be necessary at the trial'. On 10 June Douglas and Shaw reseized her 'in order that they may come in for a share of the seizure in the event of the vessel being condemned. In the meantime, however, the parties agree that the seizure should be returned by the collector but in the event of a trail ...' At this stage she was valued at £140.

On 23 June 1791 the collector commented on a petition from Steven Martin, the master, 'both Mr Douglas and Mr Carmichael have identified her and are ready to make oath that she is the same vessel which they saw at Battlehill on the morning of Friday the 13th of May last, when and where she delivered her cargo. We can have no difficulty therefore in stating that the petition is not founded in fact. At least it appears so to us with regard to the number of hands a board when the vessel was seized. We believe it true that she was poorly manned because the collector and comptroller of Whitehaven write us there were only four hands including the master [Martin] and another, who called himself only a passenger, when she came in and was detained in that port.'

The collector then wrote to both Carmichael and Douglas, asking them for the proof - to Carmichael 'PS as Robert Ostle was at the boat and in view of the vessel during the discharge you will send him here that we may hear what he can prove' and to Douglas 'PS did you see any prohibited goods carried from aboard of the vessel or what other mode of proof can you offer that a discharge of contraband goods was actually made from said vessel at the time mentioned?'

In December 1791 the *Betsey*, which had been appraised at £5 10s, was exposed for sale but 'no persons appeared who would give the appraised value'. As a result she was re-exposed for sale and this time she was purchased and in January 1792 she was registered de novo at Dumfries.

The *Mayflower* of Larne (registered at Wigtown in 1786)
In September 1789 David Douglas had information 'respecting a vessel, who had smuggled her cargo at Powfoot, being at Browhouses.' This information was passed on to Carmichael but he and his crew were 'from home'. As a result on 30 September the collector sent 'herewith Baldwin Martin and John Stothart'. In the meantime Douglas and Geddis had seized her and a second letter to Carmichael desired him 'upon your arrival [to] lose no time in proceeding to bring her round accordingly and as we have also learned that she has been very much stripped of her rigging and sails. You will endeavour to procure as many of these as you may think will be necessary to bring her round.

'PS you will desire Mr Douglas to do his endeavours to procure and detain the vessel's register or if Mr Douglas should not be there when you go you will do your endeavours to do so.'

On 2 October the collector wrote to Douglas per express reporting what they had done to give him assistance, adding 'in the mean time should you have occasion for more, there is a recruiting party at Annan, which you may command, as also several constables. You will take the earliest opportunity of doing your [best] endeavours to procure and detain the vessel's register and the books you mention are no doubt as subject to seizure as the sloop ...'

At the end of November the sloop was returned to the Board as seizure No 7 with a supposed value £40 or £50, together with the account of expenses of seizing and securing her amounting to £6 6s 3d. When the sloop was officially appraised, she was found to be valued at only £15 10s. The collector's explanation was dated 30 December 'your Honours will please to know that the limits of this port extends about thirty miles on each side of Dumfries and [it was] at one of those extremities that the seizure of the *Mayflower* was made. She now lies at Carsethorn a distance of fourteen or fifteen miles from here and has not been nearer since she was seized. This being the case we had of ourselves no opportunity of ascertaining her real value. We applied to Mr Carmichael, under whose care she then lay, but he could not give the necessary information.'

The *Mayflower* was exposed for sale on 15 February 1790 but there were no offers for her. On 26 March 1790 she was purchased to be broken up by John Martin junior in Preston (see Chapter Three).

The *Neptune* of Carlisle

On 31 December 1793 the Board informed Dumfries 'The sloop Neptune of Carlisle, John Patton master, cleared out the 14th inst at Port Glasgow with 56 hogsheads [of] tobacco for Ostend, put in on the 19th at the port of Stranraer to get some damage repaired, sailed from thence on the 20th and was seen on the 24th from the hulk at Drummore, in the Bay of Luce, hovering on the coast. From which circumstance and from information received that this vessel about three months ago cleared out from Liverpool with a cargo of tobacco for Bergen but relanded the same by another vessel, commanded by one Agnew, at Sarkfoot ... there is reason to suspect her present cargo is likewise intended to be relanded in this kingdom.

'I have the commissioners directions to signify the same to you in case the said vessel shall put into your port. And that from the time of her arrival and from examination of the persons on board there shall be reason to presume she has not performed her voyage to Ostend but relanded her cargo of tobacco in this kingdom she may be detained and notice given of her arrival and detention and other circumstances respecting her to this Board.'

In February 1794 the Board in London requested 'that endeavours may be used to procure the necessary affidavits in regard to transhipping and relanding out of the said vessel a cargo of tobacco which is said to have been shipped on board of her at Liverpool in or out of her at sea into another vessel, commanded by one Agnew, by which the tobacco was relanded at Sarkfoot ... I ... direct you to use your utmost endeavours to obtain affidavits ... and to obtain information of the facts and circumstances relative thereto and of the persons who were concerned therein or are in condition to prove the same, reporting the result to this port [Liverpool]'.

There was a request on 14 April 'to hasten as much as the case will admit of your answer ...'

In the meantime 'she [the *Neptune*] having appeared at Annan Waterfoot on the 14th April 1794 with a cargo of slates the collector immediately wrote Mr McConnochie of the king's boat to attend him in order that he might give him orders to detain the vessel in case it should be judged proper ... On the 16th April the master of the *Neptune* came to the custom house and being examined orders were given to detain the vessel ...'

On 24 April the Board in Edinburgh had 'received particular information that the tobacco shipped on board the [*Neptune*] ... at Port Glasgow in December [1793] was on or about the 25th of that month transhipped at sea upon the coast of Donaghadee ... into boats which relanded it in this kingdom, part of it at Sarkfoot ... the ... vessel being forfeited for relanding the tobacco by the Act 29 Geo 3 Cap 68 Sec 46, the Board therefore direct that she be seized by the collector for that cause and a return thereof made by him in which the officers share is to be declared to be subject to the Board. You are at the same time to transmit to the Board the certificate of registry in order that it may be retained till the issue of the prosecution of the vessel and may then be disposed of as shall be proper. With regard to the deposition of the master and mate, taken by the collector ... the Board commend the pains he has bestowed on this examination and they direct that he do likewise examine the rest of the ship's company as to both or either of the voyages on which they shall be respectively found to have served, if he can possibly get them to come before him for examination. He should also endeavour to obtain proof of the landing of part of the cargo of tobacco out of this vessel at Sarkfoot in December last ...'

The *Neptune* was condemned in the Exchequer to be sold and the collector wrote on 11 July 1794 'I cannot help thinking however that selling the vessel under the conditions of the hull being broken up will be attended with a considerable disadvantage to the revenue, as well as to the seizure makers. You will observe by her register she is quite new and is so well found in all her materials that I am persuaded she will either sell as a merchant vessel or for His Majesty's service for £350 or £400. And several merchants have already been enquiring about her. I wish therefore you would be so good as to state the matter to the commissioners and see if they will consent to sell her entire for I think it a pity that so much money should be lost to all concerned.

'In June 1791 the *Betsey*, burthen about 56 tons, smuggled a quantity of tobacco and other articles into this port and was seized, brought to condemnation and afterwards sold entire. The *Neptune* is a much more valuable vessel ...'

The Board agreed and in July 1794 the *Neptune* was sold for £410 to Robert McDowall 'who after the sale laid down £12 10s, part of the deposit of 25%, and said he would go and immediately bring the remainder of the deposit. And in a short time returned and said he found it would be impossible for him to pay the remainder of the deposit before the 23rd or 24th ult [July] ... [but] the purchaser had not appeared or remitted the remainder of the deposit and ... if the remainder of the price at which the vessel was purchased is not paid up within 20 days from the day of sale the £12 10s paid in part by the purchaser is to be considered as forfeited and the vessel exposed of anew to sale and the said £12 10s is to be added to the price she then sells for and the two sums deemed the value of the vessel and to be mentioned as such in the certificate of sale.'

The *Neptune* was advertised in the Dumfries Weekly Journal to be re-exposed to sale on Wednesday, 3rd September 1794. This time she was sold to John Little.

This is not the end of the story. In July 1795 Andrew Taylor and the other boatmen belonging to the king's boat at Carsethorn petitioned for a share in the seizure money. But the collector was the seizure maker he only gave over the care of the vessel to McConnochie and his crew 'and this is mentioned to show the impropriety, not to use a harsher term, of the petitioners stating that they were the seizure makers'.

The *Flora*

In February 1788 the collector wrote to Mr Bruce, commander of the king's boat at Carsethorn, 'We have just now received information that the smuggling cutter *Flora* is at present on the Galloway coast. Part of her cargo has been landed at Abbeyburn and a seizure made of 47 ankers there by the Kirkcudbright officers. On Sunday night she was seen towards dark lying off Barholm, where it is supposed a great quantity of goods must have been landed. And we are of opinion that the boat's crew and tidesmen may make a considerable seizure about Balcary and Colvend and therefore hope you will immediately upon receipt of this lose no time in setting out for these parts, taking with you James Hunter and Samuel Wilson, tidesmen. And upon this occasion we particularly request an exertion of your attention and activity, having no doubt if these are exerted but a considerable seizure may be made.'

The *Flora* and her cargo also escaped on the next occasion. The collector at Stranraer reported to the Board in November 1790 that 'during a search of two days nothing was got by way of the officers of customs or excise. That upon the return of the collector's clerk, who had gone to Auchinmalg to endeavour to fall in with some goods, on the night of the 25th you sent an express to the *Pilote* and the *Royal George* cutters as also the *Porcupine* frigate, all in Loch Ryan, and acquainted them of the smuggler having part of her cargo on board and pointed out to them

Figure 9: An Eighteenth Century Smuggler

such places as you thought they were most likely to fall in with her. And you having by a postscript to your said letter signified that since writing the above you are informed the same smuggling cutter returned the 25th and discharged the remainder of her cargo at Auchinmalg, the cutters mentioned notwithstanding the intelligence sent still remained in the mouth of Loch Ryan. I am directed to acquaint you that the *Royal George* being at this time under the command of Mr Ritchie the mate you are to give him the said matter in charge ...'

Figure 7 shows the *Flora* chased by three revenue cutters, but not in Scotland.

Finally there is the tale of Captain Yawkins, who was the role model for Scott's Dirk Hatteraick in 'Guy Mannering'. The letter from Kirkcudbright was found in the Liverpool letter-book extracts.

In June 1787 the collector at Liverpool, on instructions from Edinburgh, wrote to the Board in London, enclosing a letter from Kirkcudbright, dated 22 June. 'On Saturday night last, the 16th inst, about teno'clock a great deal of firing was heard at sea off the Abbey Burn in this district. We were soon after informed that a smuggling lugger was taken by one of the admiralty cruisers and have since made all the enquiry in our power into the particulars. The lugger appeared off Abbey Burn late in the evening of the 16th inst and her cargo was certainly intended to be smuggled at that place, for a boat brought on shore seventeen boxes of tea out of her, which were immediately carried off, a numerous body of horsemen being in waiting. The lugger was taken by the cruiser, whose name is the *Pilote* cutter, Lieutenant Warwick Oben, commander, within a league or a league and a half of the Abbey Burn and carried to Liverpool where she arrived on Tuesday last the 19th inst. The lugger had on board when she was taken, according to our information, between eighty and ninety boxes of tea, four hundred ankers of spirits and a quantity of silks and tobacco being the most valuable cargo of contraband goods which for many years past has appeared upon this coast. We submit to Your Honours that from the circumstances we have stated this vessel and cargo ought to be brought back to some port in Scotland and returned to you for condemnation.

'PS Since writing the above we are informed that the lugger was commanded by the noted Yawkins and that she was loaded at Ostend.'

The collector at Kirkcudbright was clearly not successful because in August 1787 there is a Liverpool letter reporting to London 'Captain Gibson, commander of the *Perseus* frigate, a vessel employed for the suppression of smuggling on the coasts of this and adjoining counties, declines to receive the *Hawke* lugger [Yawkins's lugger] as a tender to the *Perseus*. We have therefore directed her to be broken up pursuant to your commands.'

This did not deter Yawkins. On 12 August 1789 the Board wrote to the collector 'We have received your letter of the 4th inst stating the proceedings of Mr Oliphant, tidesurveyor, Mr Stewart, commander of the *Justice* hulk, and the officers under their survey in watching the lugger commanded by [Jack] Yawkins, so as to prevent her from landing any part of her cargo on the coast, which vessel has been captured and carried into Liverpool by Captain Burges of His Majesty's sloop *Savage*, who sailed in quest of her, in consequence of information from the collector. And submitting an account of the severe duty the officers and military were subjected to on this occasion that they may be allowed a gratuity out of the seizure. We acquaint you that though the services stated are very commendable and what we much approve of, they are only such as come within the line of their duty.'

The next chapter concentrates on the individuals who were involved in the smuggling.

CHAPTER EIGHT: SMUGGLERS - THE MEN

'Re charge against Christopher Armstrong, relating to the seizure of the sloop *Nancy* of Stranraer at the Hagg on the 24th October ... [his] answers [must have been] prepared by some person of more knowledge than himself. But though a great deal of ingenuity has been exerted on the occasion, we are still of our former opinion that he acted improperly. He has in his defence attempted to criminate some very deserving officers and charged them with negligence in not going to his assistance, which we know to be false. His messages arrived at the custom house at four o'clock of the afternoon and the comptroller, surveyor and landwaiter set off with all possible dispatch to his assistance. But the distance being upwards of seven miles and some miles of the road very bad they did not arrive at the place where the vessel had been lying till about seven o'clock, when they saw nothing of her but learned from people living on the shore that she had gone off with the tide some time before. And night being then set in they could obtain no further intelligence of Armstrong or the sloop till next morning, when they observed the vessel lying on a bank on the other side of the river. In regard to the claim he now sets up for the thirty-one bags of salt seized in Mrs Coid's house by the other officers and for which he produces a certificate by Isabel Coid, we believe it to be perfectly unfounded and the certificate fabricated for the purpose. For the girl denies having any knowledge of such certificate or its contents. And further he made no claim for the thirty-one bags salt for fourteen days after he had returned the seizure of the sloop and eight bags salt. Upon the whole therefore we think his answers are more calculated to criminate the other officers than exculpate himself and from the knowledge we have of the various circumstances attending this business we cannot help stating it as our opinion that his conduct in regard to his duty has been ignorant and improper ...' (Collector at Dumfries to the Board, 5 December 1805). Note: The Coids were smugglers.

The Collector and the Smuggler

'The collector having occasion to go down to Arbigland on Sunday last [31 July 1786] Mr Craik and him observing a vessel lying off Southerness Point, which they took no particular notice of, imagining she was a sloop coming up the river with coals or lime. And on the Monday morning she was observed in the same place, notwithstanding she might have gone up with the foregoing night tide. This occasioning a little suspicion and a four oared boat being observed alongside of her, the collector went down to Southerness. And having hailed the vessel the captain or commander came ashore, seeming very much the worse of liquor. And in his conversation told the collector that the vessel lying off was tender to the cutter now stationed on the coast of Galloway and commanded by Captain Cook. That he had chased a smuggling boat the night before but from his want of knowledge of the channel she had escaped by his running aground. The tide being then making the collector offered to procure him a pilot who could conduct him with great safety up any part of the channel. And accordingly dispatched a tidesman attending to Carsethorn, who having returned with a pilot the captain behaved with great rudeness to him. And notwithstanding every remonstrance by the collector against such conduct, it only served to increase the fellow's abuse, which indeed the collector imputed to his drunkenness at the time rather than what turned out afterwards to be the case.

'In this abusive ill humour the captain took his boat and went aboard. And the collector was informed that he had about fifteen hands with as many swivels etc. And on returning to Arbigland and reflecting on the business, he from several circumstances began to be confident that the story of the tender was false and that he might be a smuggler. No boat or vessel was near however to attempt to go aboard her. And indeed under such circumstances it would have been very hazardous without a considerable force of men and arms. But to be more satisfied as to her quality and views the collector went over to Carsethorn to endeavour to learn whether any such vessel had been discovered passing that way in the foregoing tide, which was full about two o'clock in the morning. Luckily he received information that a vessel with a boat answering her description was seen to pass down about three or four o'clock. And that she seemed to have come from a place called Lantonside on the other side of the river from Carsethorn and nearly opposite to it. The pretended tender's quality and business being now pretty well ascertained the collector set off instantly for Dumfries and having mustered a party of officers etc proceeded directly towards the place where it was suspected the smuggled goods were deposited. The collector accompanied the party to within two miles of the Lantonside but from the fatigue he had in the former part of the day he was so much knocked up that he could not proceed. The party, however, being put under the direction of the landsurveyor and landwaiter went forward to the place and found thirty-eight packages of tobacco weighing 4,359 lbs, which is now safely lodged in the custom house and we now inclose your Honours a return of the seizure accordingly.

'As the pretended tender continued in her station off Southerness, when the collector left Carsethorn on Monday evening, and as from that circumstance it might be suspected she had more business to do before she left that part of the coast, he sent off an express to the collector and comptroller of the customs at Kirkcudbright, informing them of the occurrence and requesting if Captain Cook was in their neighbourhood that they might communicate the same to him without delay so as he might take the necessary measures for securing his pretended friend. We are sorry, however, to understand by a letter from the collector and comptroller at Kirkcudbright that Captain Cook was not in the neighbourhood. And therefore we fear the smuggler will make his escape ... the size or burthen of the smuggler seems about 20 or 25 tons. And with regard to the tobacco seized it was done in the [nick of] time for before the party had secured the possession about eight or nine carts were very near the spot to carry it off ...'

This smuggler sounds like a rough character, the archetypal smuggler of fiction and folklore. However, in the majority of cases the smugglers were the ordinary people. These can be identified in the letter-books and some have been selected in the following Smugglers A to Z.

Joseph Brough, John Lands and John Henderson

Joseph Brough was a ferryman living in Whinnyrigg. In November 1818 he was involved in smuggling, apparently for the first time. The following statement was taken by John Dalgleish, the Principal Coast Officer at Annan. 'He distinctly states and declares that he does not know whether John Lands and John Henderson put the whole of the whisky on board the boat, as he did not know that they were there until he went on board and found them there. And he immediately quarrelled [with] them for being there and enquired if the spirits also belonged to them, when they answered the bloke over there when they came to the boat. And they did not know to whom they belonged as the tins only belonged to them. And he distinctly declares he does not know who put the casks of whisky into the boat, as he neither heard of any body claiming them nor did he see any body putting them there. Nor does he know by what conveyance either the casks or the tins were put into the boat. For he had been crossing the water to Bowness in the night before and had missed his night's rest and had gone to bed about eight o'clock in the evening the boat and whisky were seized and had requested his wife to call him up after ten o'clock in the evening to ferry over the Solway two gentlemen from Keswick. When he arose and went to the boat and found John Lands and John Henderson in the boat as before stated.'

John Lands was a fisherman in Sandhills and John Henderson a stocking man in Annan. They were both charged in the penalty of £200 for smuggling whisky. Henderson was arrested and sent to the tollbooth at Annan. In March 1821 the collector reported to Dalgleish that the Treasury were 'pleased to authorise [his] release ... on his finding security in £50 not to be again concerned in smuggling. We request you will call on him to know two persons who are willing to be security for him, the individual suffficing of whom for the said sum you are to report to us for the information of the Honourable Board.' Richard Graham and James Little, both of Annan, agreed to give the bond for an indefinite period.

John Lands had succeeded in evading capture and in April 1821 the collector reported to the Board's solicitor 'we have made private enquiry as to the present place of abode of John Lands ... and we find that he lives now generally on the Cumberland side of the Firth and that he is occasionally seen on this side at Sandhills, where his wife still resides in the house he formerly inhabited.' They were instructed to enquire into his circumstances and reported in May 'we find that he is possessed of no effects, except some household furniture of little value, and that as far as we can learn his circumstances are bad and quite unable to pay the penalty ...'

In September 1822 Dalgleish reported 'I beg leave to inform you that John Lands ... is now going at large in this side of the Solway. George Brown and I saw him here today.' Lands was arrested.

In the meantime the collector wrote on 19 November 1821 to John Little, merchant, and Robert Elliott, glazier, both of Annan 'We received your letter of the 15th inst informing us of the insolvency of Joseph Brough at Whinnyrigg, owner of the boat *Ann* of Annan, licensed at this port on the 23rd February 1820. And intimating to us a wish to be relieved as his sureties in the bond entered into by you and him of the above date for the licence then delivered to him for the use of the boat. In answer we have to acquaint you that your request in this case cannot be complied with and you must continue his sureties until the boat is sold, lost or otherwise destroyed.'

The Kennedy Killing (and William Farish)
In May 1789 the collector and comptroller at Kirkcudbright received an express from Dumfries. 'It is with much concern we inform you that this morning about five o'clock the king's boat stationed at Carsethorn fell in with a smuggling cutter off Skinburness, who refused to strike. And having fired into the king's boat killed one man and dangerously wounded another. After this the boat returned to Carsethorn and the smuggler proceeded up the Firth towards the Border. We have now dispatched a party of officers etc to the Border by land and the [king's] boat is to endeavour to intercept the smuggler returning down the Firth. The collector of excise has sent an express to the captain of the king's cutter stationed at Balcary to hurry him out to the assistance of Carmichael. And this goes to you by express to request you may communicate the information to Captain Cook, in case he or any of his people should be in your neighbourhood. Inclosed is a description of the smuggler, several of whose hands are well known to Carmichael's crew.'

Witnesses were interviewed in May and June when 'three additional witnesses viz George Carruthers, Andrew Irving and John Forsyth (who formerly kept out of the way) having since voluntarily presented themselves and been examined by the sheriff ... Andrew Irving has very evidently prevaricated and withheld his knowledge of the facts but when he comes before a court he will probably recollect better what passed at the different interviews he had with the crew of the smuggler and also who the two strangers were. George Carruthers junior in Hollandbush, Thomas Wyllie in Stock and James Weal in Browhouses were present and assisted at the discharge of the smuggler and of course must know the hands on board of her. They were summoned by the sheriff substitute when down on the Border taking the precognition to appear as witnesses but refused to attend as they were aiding and assisting in the smuggle. If they are included in the proclamation it will at least bring them forward as witnesses.'

Simon McKenzie, writer, charged £28 5s 8d for his services, which was paid on 26 April 1790.

William Farish was also involved in this. He was well-known to the officers at Dumfries. In December 1784 he had retaliated against George Halliday and Andrew Smith for seizing his boat the *Jean and Betty* and a load of coals by charging them with everything from trespass to improper conduct. The correspondence continued for several months as customs refused to return the boat until Farish agreed to drop the charges against the tidesmen.

On 28 May 1785 the collector wrote directly to Farish at Annan 'We request to know whether you are willing to discharge the action commenced at your instance against Andrew Smith and George Halliday, tidesmen, and to grant a release of all claim of costs and damages on account of the seizure or re-seizure of your wherry *Jean and Betty* and pay the expenses incurred in consequence of the re-seizure of her in case the Board shall be pleased to agree with your request and order the vessel to be delivered up.'

And on 19 November 1785 'We desire to know whether upon re-delivering your wherry formerly seized by George Halliday and Andrew Smith ... you will oblige yourself not to prosecute them for expenses or damages upon its being agreed not to insist for payment from you of the charges incurred by the officers at re-seizing said wherry. Your answer in course is expected.'

The wherry was returned to Farish in December.

On 1 June 1789 the collector wrote 'It appears that one William Farish (who on a former occasion gave us a great deal of trouble about a parcel of coals which it was alleged he had smuggled) had been active in persuading Andrew Irving to get out of the way. This is really [a] matter of much concern, as Irving would have been a most material witness as to the whole crew aboard the smuggler. For [as] he attended her the whole night and part of the morning of Thursday of course he must have known well who was aboard. And it is said that in his boat he carried some additional hands to the smuggler from an apprehension she might fall in with the king's boat. It would be well therefore since he does not choose to appear as an evidence and since Farish has been so active in the business that they could both be conjoined with the crew of the smuggler in the prosecution as aiding and assisting. We shall be at every pains to procure what further evidence we can relative to the persons concerned in this disagreeable affair ...'

Richard Graham, James Land and Charles Lyme

On 15 November 1784 the collector at Whitehaven reported on petition of Richard Graham of Torduff. 'We are well informed the petitioner is in good circumstances, that he keeps an entered spirit cellar at Torduff, and has been notoriously concerned in smuggling for many years past ... Charles Lyme (Syme?), master of the boat and alleged to have escaped from the constables and fled the country, is a near relation of the petitioner. James Land, mariner, has been employed by the Scotch smugglers as pilot in bringing up the Solway Firth to the Scotch borders smuggling vessels for these ten years past. We enclose a copy of a letter this day received from John Lawson the seizing officer and from every circumstance of the case we have reason to believe the salt was shipped by direction of the petitioner with intention to be smuggled, and we further observe that if the boat and salt were delivered to the petitioner it would a great inlet to frauds and a standing precedent for future applications when seizures were made.'

Richard Hetherton

Hetherton was the smuggler who was involved in the case against Geddis and Elliott in the previous chapter (and in 'Family Histories in Scottish Customs Records'). In 1806 the collector was concerned about his ownership of the sloop *Speedwell*. This vessel was originally registered at Beaumaris and apparently sold by John Hughes to Richard Hetherton. But the bill of sale was 'suspected of being a fabrication'. Despite several letters to the collector and comptroller at Liverpool, there is no evidence that any fraud was proved.

Robert McDowall

It is still unclear whether or not there were two Robert McDowalls in the records or whether one moved from Sarkfoot to Annan during the period under review.

Robert McDowall of Sarkfoot

There are frequent references to the new company of smugglers at Sarkfoot run by McDowall & Co. On 2 August 1786 the collector wrote 'We have been informed of late that several carrying boats ... have been observed passing up the Firth towards Leehouses and Sarkfoot. And at the latter place we understand a smuggling company have established themselves under pretence of carrying on a fair trade. To these and other places on that part of the coast the tobacco, spirits etc are carried and from thence through the country to the northern counties of England. This day we have had an information of a smuggler about ten days ago from Guernsey to Jersey direct to the company (McDowall & Co) at Sarkfoot consisting of 100 packages of tobacco and a good deal of spirits. The vessel was about 25 tons burthen ...'

On 10 July 1786 'Robert McDowall at Sarkfoot ... about twenty-eight miles from this, came here and produced a sufferance and cocket from Wigtown for 99 bushels small salt, one pipe of wine, 13 cwt sugar and one puncheon containing 114 gallons rum. The salt, sugar and rum we granted a warrant of discharge for but the wine being unaccompanied with the usual certificate of the payment of the duties and the oath of identity we did not think it proper to grant warrant of discharge ... but judged it more proper to secure it till we laid the matter before your Honours. We therefore sent down for that purpose the comptroller's clerk together with George Halliday, tidesman, (Mr Twaddel landwaiter being busy engaged on foreign ships). Next day the comptroller's clerk returned having secured it. By the sufferance from Wigtown it mentions the wine having been imported there in the *Countess of Galloway* from Oporto the 2nd June 1785 and the duties paid by Robert Murray. The sufferance is granted for 126 gallons, John Hannah landwaiter endorses on the same 140 gallons and the cocket is for that quantity. We beg leave your Honours will be pleased to give us such directions concerning it as you shall see proper.'

Before a reply had been received, on 15 July 1786 'Robert McDowall came to the custom house and produced to us the inclosed certificate for the above pipe of wine, containing 140 gallons, and represented that it was an entire oversight in the merchant who sent it to him and desired we would deliver him up the pipe as no fraud was intended or committed. Upon which we acquainted him that the matter was laid before your Honours and could not be returned till we had directions ...'

The Board authorised the return of the wine to Robert Murray in August 1786. But this started deep suspicions about the *Countess of Galloway*. When she arrived at Sarkfoot in October 1787, David Douglas was instructed to attend the discharge of her wine. He sent Mr Twaddel but was instructed to go as well.

In 1789 there was a detailed enquiry into a shipment of twelve dozen bottles of Portugal wine on the *Countess of Galloway*. But she could not be seized because, as reported on 19 June she had 'sailed from this river on Sunday last and we are informed got round to Wigtown on Monday the 15th inst.' They asked the collector and comptroller at Wigtown how many bottles of wine were on board when she arrived there and were defeated by the answer: none.

Robert McDowall of (Hopses) Annan
This Robert McDowall was a fish curer and a smuggler. When Robert Carmichael, commander of the king's boat at Carsethorn, was charged with collusion in 1791 (see previous chapter) the collector suggested to him 'as a good deal of stress has been laid by Mr Douglas upon a conversation that passed betwixt you and Mr Robert McDowall in Hopses I submit to you if you ought not to summon him as a witness.'

When Carmichael failed to bring him forward as a witness, the collector wrote to McDowall direct 'Wishing to ask you a few questions respecting the seizure made by Mr Carmichael ... I have to request you will come up here for that purpose on Saturday or Monday next, when you shall be detained only a very short time. And if you do not come in this way I will be under the necessity of bringing you by diligence. And you will with your earliest convenience inform me by post upon which day you intend to come.'

In his report to the Board, dated 3 October 1791, the collector commented 'On the charge of making a collusive seizure I would beg leave to observe that no direct proof of this fact has appeared. Mr Carmichael has brought forward two of his hands in the boat ... to prove that no collusion could take place ... but the fact is as sworn to by Mr Robert McDowall, one of the reputed owners of the cargo ... that he was in company and in conversation for about five minutes on the evening that the smuggling vessel was discharged at Battlehill with Mr Carmichael at Annan and at the very place mentioned by Mr Elliot's examination in support of the charge.

'Mr McDowall could not recollect any part of the conversation on that occasion with Mr Carmichael but knew that the seizure of fifteen casks gin was made and believes it was deposited in the place where seized for that purpose and that he had reason to believe that information thereof was given to Joseph Irving now deceased one of Mr Carmichael's hands and that he has no doubt Mr Carmichael was informed thereof but that no collusive bargain was made with Mr Carmichael by any of the owners if the said cargo to his knowledge.'

The Board were anxious that Carmichael should be dismissed but when the collector discovered that McDowall was in town 'It was proposed by Mr Carmichael and his agent to examine Mr McDowall ... his deposition ... appearing more favourable for Mr Carmichael than his former evidence, particularly his answer to the last interrogatory, we have ventured to delay putting the Honourable Board's orders into execution for a day or two until Mr McDowall's evidence has been under consideration and till the pleasure of your Honours is further known. Your Honours will observe from a perusal of McDowall's evidence that an interrogatory was put whether McDowall attended on his former examination in consequence of a citation or of a letter from the collector desiring his attendance and that the fact being that the collector for the sake of saving expenses had desired his attendance by a letter we at the collector's desire inclose a copy of the said letter [see above] ...'

In February 1791 Robert McDowall purchased at Whitehaven the sloop *Mary*, registered at Barnstaple in 1787 and subsequently condemned for smuggling. Within days McDowall sold the sloop to William Breckenridge of Dowhill, Ayrshire, another known smuggler. In 1794 McDowall attempted to purchase the *Neptune* but could not afford the £410.

In July 1796 the collector commented in his salt account that Robert McDowall had become a bankrupt and that his trustee had declined giving the necessary bond.

Robert McDowall and William Lowes of the *Peggy*

This letter comes from the Whitehaven letter-books. On 3 December 1783 the collector reported to the Board in London on the petition of William Lowes, sole owner and master of an open boat called the *Peggy*. He bought six tons potatoes at the Water of Urr to take to Flimby. While in Scotland, he was approached by William McWilliams, Robert McDowall and Robert McGir, who asked for a passage to England. But they did not inform Lowes that they had brought any goods on board his boat. When they were halfway over the water towards Flimby, he discovered a keg almost covered with potatoes, 'which he expressed great surprise at, and asked the said passengers what it was, when they told him it was brandy, and your petitioner was very angry with them and attempted to turn back to Scotland. But the wind proved unfavourable for their return.'

They landed in Flimby Bay about three o'clock the next morning and 'after mooring the boat your petitioner and his passengers went to his house, which was very near, for some refreshment. And when they returned to the boat, which was in about half an hour, they found His Majesty's officers of the customs there, who had found and seized amongst the potatoes seven kegs of brandy, which had been concealed there wholly unknown to your petitioner ... And that the said McWilliams, McDowall and McGir, on finding that the officers had seized the brandy, immediately ran to a hedge which was near, and got each a stake thereout to beat the officers with and threatened to kill them if they did not immediately give up the brandy. When the officers desired your petitioner to prevail on the said men to desist from carrying their threats into execution and to protect them if possible until morning and told your petitioner it should be better for him, when your petitioner accordingly, with great difficulty, prevailed on the said McWilliams, McDowall and McGir to be quiet. Your petitioner stayed by the officers at their request till seven o'clock in the morning, when the officers took the brandy to the custom house at Workington, and seized your petitioner's boat. That your petitioner and ... [the] officers verily believe that if your petitioner had not interfered ... the ... smugglers would have either killed the officers or rescued the ... brandy from them, they being very strong and resolute men. That your petitioner is but twenty-five years of age and has a wife who is blind and lost the use of her limbs from a late severe illness and five small children and your petitioner is so poor ...'

The Radcliffs

There were three Radcliffs, Anthony the father and Jonathan and Anthony the sons. They were fish curers who were deeply involved in salt smuggling. As a result their names occur frequently throughout the salt accounts of the 1780s and 1790s. Anthony Radcliff's sloop the *Grizel* was also involved in tobacco smuggling.

John Scott, George Irving and James Goldie

In June 1780 an assault was committed by John Scott, George Irving and James Goldie on Robert Johnstone officer of excise and Baldwin Martin, tidesman. The sheriff issued warrants for their arrest and in July Francis Short, messenger, produced two accounts, totalling £47 16s 1d for his trouble and expenses in arresting Scott and Irving. The Board's comment was 'we think proper to return the said accounts to you and to signify that the charges appearing much too high we are desirous of the opinion of Mr Aiken procurator fiscal at Dumfries as to the propriety thereof, which you are to request in our name that this matter may be properly settled.'

The matter was finally settled in June 1784, when it was agreed that Short actually spent £23 4s 7d. He was entitled to three years and eight months interest on that sum, being £4 4s 0d. And that instead of twenty guineas charged by him for trouble a guinea a day for the eight days he was employed was a sufficient allowance, being £8 8s 0d. He was paid £35 16s 7d.

In the meantime Irving, Scott and Goldie were prosecuted and tried.

John Scott and the death of Joseph Wilson
Once again it is unclear whether or not the John Scott referred to here is the same as the one above. As this one clearly lived at Balcary, it is doubtful.

In December 1780 the collector at Whitehaven wrote to the Board in London 'Yesterday we were informed (but not officially) therefore could not with certainty acquaint your Honours thereof, that Joseph Wilson, tidesman at Workington, was killed on board the king's boat in attempting to board a smuggling cutter then hovering off that port - the particular explanations relating that affair ... we received this morning from the Justices clerk. And have further to observe that John Scott therein mentioned, who is a most notorious smuggler, has been sent to the county gaol under strong guard of constables and militia, for fear of a rescue (there being a number of smugglers upon the coast) on a commitment for loitering ... at the request of Mr Lutwidge and the other magistrates, also of the coroner, who has adjourned the jury upon the inquest and view of the body till his return. We have sent over John Dixon tidesman (who took Scott upon the boat) to Balcary in Scotland, the place of Scott's residence, to enquire after two other persons mentioned by him in his examination, who are supposed to be concerned in the affair. He has direction also to make any further enquiries necessary so that any of the other offenders may be brought to justice. Upon his return we shall transmit your Honours the circumstantial account of the whole affair and have further to observe there is great reason to hope James Burrow, the other officer wounded, may recover, the ball having grazed upon his head and taken off part of his ear, but not certain whether or not there is any fracture in the skull.'

John Dixon returned from Scotland six days later with examinations of the two persons referred to by Scott 'supposed to be concerned in the murder of Joseph Wilson ... Scott having refused to sign his declaration, which himself afterwards contradicted and appears to be false, in every instance except as to his landing and the names of the two persons which brought him over ...' On 29 December 1780 the collector was able to report the verdict of the coroner 'wilful murder by some person or persons, having shot the deceased through the head with a musket or blunderbuss from out of a smuggling sloop on the high seas near Workington. We also inclose copy of the examination of Scott ... which he refused to sign ... Also of Iere Thompson relating to that affair from what as yet appeared we are apprehensive no material proof has been yet obtained to justify Scott's detainer in prison for that offence.'

Scott was discharged in February 1781 and the customs expenses, presumably including the trip to Scotland, were £34 0s 8 1/2d.

John Wyllie of Leehouses

John Wyllie lived in Lee or Leehouses. His name recurs throughout the 1780s as one of the main deforcers when officers had seized smuggled goods or were searching for them. In June 1780 Baldwin Martin, tidesman at Annan, and Robert Johnstone, excise officer, were 'in consequence of an information searching for smuggled goods at Torduff [when] they were attacked and forced out of a house by John Jest, residenter of Balcary in Galloway. And that they were upon same occasion attacked in another house at Leehouses the same day by a servant of John Wyllie's at that place ...'

In December 1782 a wherry smuggled part of her cargo consisting of salt herrings, spirits and tea at Browhouses. During the search for contraband goods, John Lawson, commander of the king's boat at Skinburness, in England, and his crew were obstructed by John Wyllie and others at Wyllie's house, the Lee, and at Hollandbush. But 'it not appearing that when Mr Lawson was prevented from searching that he had any warrant or writ of assistance or any peace officer along with him he was not in that case duly authorised to enter and search houses etc' there could be no prosecution.

David Douglas, the general surveyor, and a party of soldiers were also helping with the search. The Board instructed that 'John Wyllie may be prosecuted, as also Andrew Rome for beating a soldier, who had fallen behind the party that was sent to Mr Douglas's assistance ... With respect to the prosecution proposed against John Wyllie in Lee you are to direct Mr Douglas to state the particulars he can prove against him ... with regard to the assault of one of the military. If you find there is any likelihood to ascertain the assault you are to employ the fullest person you know to apply to the sheriff of the county to cause the procurator fiscal to state the facts in a complaint ...'

In September 1785 Andrew Smith, tidesman, and Robert Johnstone, officer of excise, were deforced of several quantities of salt found by them in the houses of different persons in the neighbourhood of Browhouses by John Wyllie in Lee, Thomas Johnstone in Hollandbush and others.

A minute of the Board dated 26 April 1786 stated 'Mr Davidson, assistant solicitor, having in his memorial of the 25th laid before us a letter from Mr Archibald Campbell, the deputy advocate of the southern circuit, dated at Ayr the 31st current, returning the precognition against John Wyllie, whose trial as ordered per Minute of the 31st October 1785 came on at Dumfries on Monday the 17th instant. The jury having returned a verdict and finding the trial not proven he was assailized from the bar. And stating that he thinks it his duty to mention that the conduct of Andrew Smith, tidewaiter at Annan, who was deforced by a number of persons at Leehouses, appeared in the whole course of the business to Mr Campbell to be by no means proper. And that it would be expedient that some enquiry should be made concerning it. That the opinion he now expresses he knows to be also the opinion of Lord Broxfield, who was the judge present at the trial ...'

As late as August 1806 George Brown, tidesman at Annan, was 'strictly enjoined to keep a sharp look out upon the boat *Davies*, John Wyllie master, who was seen hasting up the Solway Firth from the lugger [a suspected smuggler, which] was last seen on the 5th and lay at the Water of Urr for eight days previous thereto without attempting to do any business ...'

This A to Z represents a mere selection of the smugglers' tales found within the pages of the letter-books. By the mid eighteenth century times had changed, as will be seen in the next chapter.

CHAPTER NINE: TOWARDS THE TWENTIETH CENTURY

(Private) 'Two Boulogne fishing luggers No 1089 and 1439 respectively have left that port bound for the coast of Scotland and Ireland and have on board seven casks of brandy and two packs of tobacco.' (Letter from the Board in London, transmitted to the Principal Coast Officer at Garlieston 1 July 1885 - CE61 5/3).

As indicated in the Chapter Two, there was a steady decline in the smuggling activity in Dumfries and Galloway so that by the mid to late nineteenth century the only recorded smuggles tend to involve small adventures with tobacco. One final suspected smuggle is quoted here from the Dumfries records for Dalbeattie.

On 28 August 1924 the coast officer at Dalbeattie wrote to Dumfries 'On Saturday morning the 23rd of August a Mr Burnett, who has a tobacco and hairdressing shop in High Street Dalbeattie, told me that a man asked him if he would buy some tobacco as he was going to try and get some from the *Chrysalis*. Mr Burnett refused to have anything to do with it. There was no quantity or price stated by this man and he was not employed on the vessel but was in touch with the men who were working on the *Chrysalis*. I have made some enquiries of Palnackie and a Mrs Nevin, who keeps a small shop there, was asked by one of the crew if she would buy a few cigarettes. Mrs Nevin refused, no quantity or price was stated. This is all the information I can get at present. The *Chrysalis* is expected back here next month.'

This was not the only evidence of tobacco smuggling from the *Chrysalis*. The same day, the Principal Officer at Dumfries reported to Ayr 'on Saturday 23rd inst the excise officer at Castle Douglas phoned me up to say that he had received an anonymous post card containing information to the effect that some tobacco had been smuggled and landed from the Chrysalis ex Bremen, which had been at Palnackie from the 7th to the 18th inst. In course of conversation he said he had what appeared to be good grounds for believing that this information was authentic ...'

One tends to feel somewhat nostalgic for the 'good old days'.

BIBLIOGRAPHY

Primary Sources
Custom House Letter-books
    West Search Room, Scottish Record Office
        CE 51 Dumfries
        CE 61 Wigtown
        CE 77 Stranraer
    Strathclyde Regional Archives
        CE 60 Port Glasgow and Greenock
        CE 76 Ayr
        CE 82 Campbeltown
    Public Record Office, Kew
        CUST82 Whitehaven
Note: Further details can be obtained from the author

Merchant Letter-books
    Manx National Heritage Library
        BH501C MIC68 George Moore letter-book 1750-1760
    Priaulx Library, St Peter Port, Guernsey
        Carteret Priaulx Letters: Lawrence Banks 24 April 1804
        Lawrence Banks 22 July 1805

Secondary Sources
Atton, Henry and Holland, Henry Hurst *The King's Customs Vol 1 An Account of Maritime Revenue and Contraband Traffic in England, Scotland and Ireland, from the earliest times to the year 1800* John Murray 1908
Chatterton, E Keble *King's Cutters and Smugglers 1700-1855* George Allen & Co 1912
Extracts from Records of the Convention of Royal Burghs 1677-1711. Published for the Convention of Royal Burghs by William Paterson, Edinburgh 1880
Jarvis, Rupert C *The Customs Cruisers of the North-west in the Eighteenth Century* Historical Society Lancs & Cheshire 97 pp41-61 1947
Jarvis, Rupert C ed *Some Records of the port of Lancaster* Transactions of the Lancashire and Cheshire Antiquarian Society Vol 58 1945-46

Shore, H N *Smuggling Days and Smuggling Ways* Castle 1892
Vyse, Charles *A New Geographical Grammar: containing a comprehensive system of modern geography after a new and curious method* London 1779

Further Reading
Gibbon, Ronald T *'To the King's Deceit'* The Friends of Whitehaven Museum 1983
Goring, Rosemary *Eighteenth-century Scottish Smugglers: The Evidence from Montrose and Dumfries* Review of Scottish Culture Issue 3 1987
Irving, Gordon *The Solway Smugglers* Robert Dinwiddie 1971
Smith, Graham *Robert Burns the Exciseman* Alloway Publishing 1989
Temperley, Alan *Tales of Galloway* Mainstream Publishing 1986
Thomson, John A *The Smuggling Coast* T C Farries & Co Ltd 1989
Wilkins, Frances *The Isle of Man in Smuggling History* Wyre Forest Press 1992
Wilkins, Frances *Strathclyde's Smuggling Story* Wyre Forest Press 1992
Wilkins, Frances *Scottish Customs and Excise Records, with particular reference to Strathclyde* Wyre Forest Press 1992
Wilkins, Frances *Family Histories in Scottish Customs Records* Wyre Forest Press 1993
Wood, J Maxwell *Smuggling in the Solway and Around the Galloway Sea-board* J Maxwell & Son Dumfries 1908

Other Primary Source Material
Dumfries Archive Centre
33 Burns Street, Dumfries DG1 2PS
0387 69254

The following information, supplied by the Archivist, is available on microfilm at the Archive Centre:

Imports and exports, port of Dumfries 1672-92 (SRO ref: E72/6/1-27)

Portpatrick Bullion Books and Collectors' accounts 1672-99 (SRO refs: E74/31/1, 2; E74/53/2-6; E73/32/14; E73/48/25; E73/70/1, 2; E73/92/1, 2; E73/113/1, 3; E73/121/14)

Bounty money paid at Portpatrick 1699 (E126/14/1, 3, 5)

Alison Bank Customs books 1666-91 (E72/2/1-23)

Alison Bank Bullion book and Collectors' accounts 1685-99 (SRO refs: E74/16/1, 2; E/74/34/1; E74/37/1-6; E73/48/3; E73/52/1-2; E73/71/3, 5; E73/96/1, 4; E73/126/5-6)

Dumfries Customs accounts - incident bills etc 1685-92 (SRO refs: E73/44/8, 9; E73/57/3/1-6; E73/79/3, 4; E73/100/6, 7; E73/100/9/1-6.

Dumfries and Kirkcudbirght Bullion accounts 1682-96 (SRO refs: E74/11/7; E74/20/1, 2; E70/34/2; E74/42/1-5)

Dumfries Port Collectors' accounts 1743-80 (SRO ref: E504/9/1-4)

Dumfries Port Collectors' accounts 1780-1830 (SRO ref: E504/9/5-10)

Portpatrick Customs accounts 1671-92 (SRO ref: E72/20/1-19)

The Archive Centre is open from 11 a.m. - 1 p.m., 2 p.m. - 5 p.m. Tuesday, Wednesday and Friday and from 6 p.m. - 9 p.m. on Thursdays. As space is limited an appointment should be made with the Archivist.

WYRE FOREST PRESS

Wyre Forest Press has been established basically to publish books on smuggling and maritime history. Forthcoming titles in 1993 include books on South Devon's Smuggling Story, Tayside's Smuggling Story, The Isle of Man's Alternative Smuggling Story, South Wales's Smuggling Story and Fife and Lothian's Smuggling Story.

Please contact the publishers for further details:

8 Mill Close, Blakedown, Kidderminster, Worcestershire DY10 3NQ